A GNOME'S GUIDE TO
CERAMICS

WRITTEN BY BECKY WEIDNER
CREATIVE DESIGN BY KARA GINTHER

PUBLISHED BY
THE WORKSHOP

COLUMBUS, WISCONSIN

NO PART OF THIS PUBLICATION MAY BE REPRODUCED, STORED IN A RETRIEVAL SYSTEM, OR TRANSMITTED IN ANY FORM OR BY ANY MEANS, ELECTRONIC, MECHANICAL, PHOTOCOPYING, RECORDING, OR OTHERWISE, WITHOUT PERMISSION OF THE AUTHOR.

FOR PERMISSION, WRITE TO THE WORKSHOP, ATTENTION: PERMISSIONS,
128 WEST JAMES STREET, COLUMBUS, WI, 53925

ISBN 978-1-7337381-1-8 (PAPERBACK)

COPYRIGHT 2024 BY REBECCA WEIDNER.
ALL RIGHTS RESERVED.

PUBLISHED BY THE WORKSHOP

DEDICATED TO THE WEDNESDAY CERAMICS CLASS AT THE WORKSHOP. —BW

BEFORE WE GET STARTED, LET'S REVIEW SOME SAFETY TIPS:

- AVOID EXCESSIVE DUST EXPOSURE FROM CLAY AND GLAZE.

- CLEAN UP WITH A MOP OR WET SPONGE.

- DO NOT EAT WHILE WORKING WITH CERAMIC MATERIALS.

- WASH TOOLS AND HANDS THOROUGHLY WHEN FINISHED WORKING.

- DO NOT WASH CLAY OR GLAZE DOWN A REGULAR SINK; INSTEAD, CLEAN UP IN A DESIGNATED BUCKET OR IN A SINK WITH A TRAP.

- FOLLOW STUDIO OR SCHOOL GUIDELINES FOR CLEAN UP.

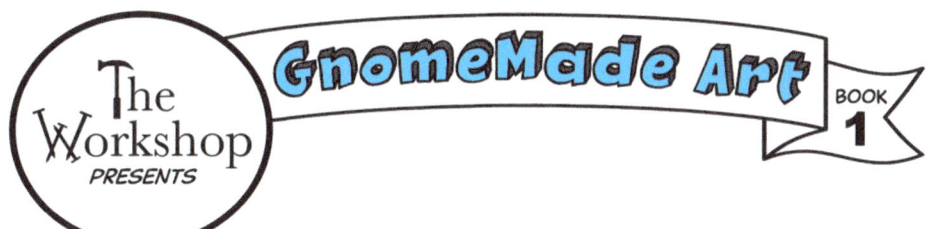

A GNOME'S GUIDE TO
CERAMICS

WRITTEN BY BECKY WEIDNER
CREATIVE DESIGN BY KARA GINTHER

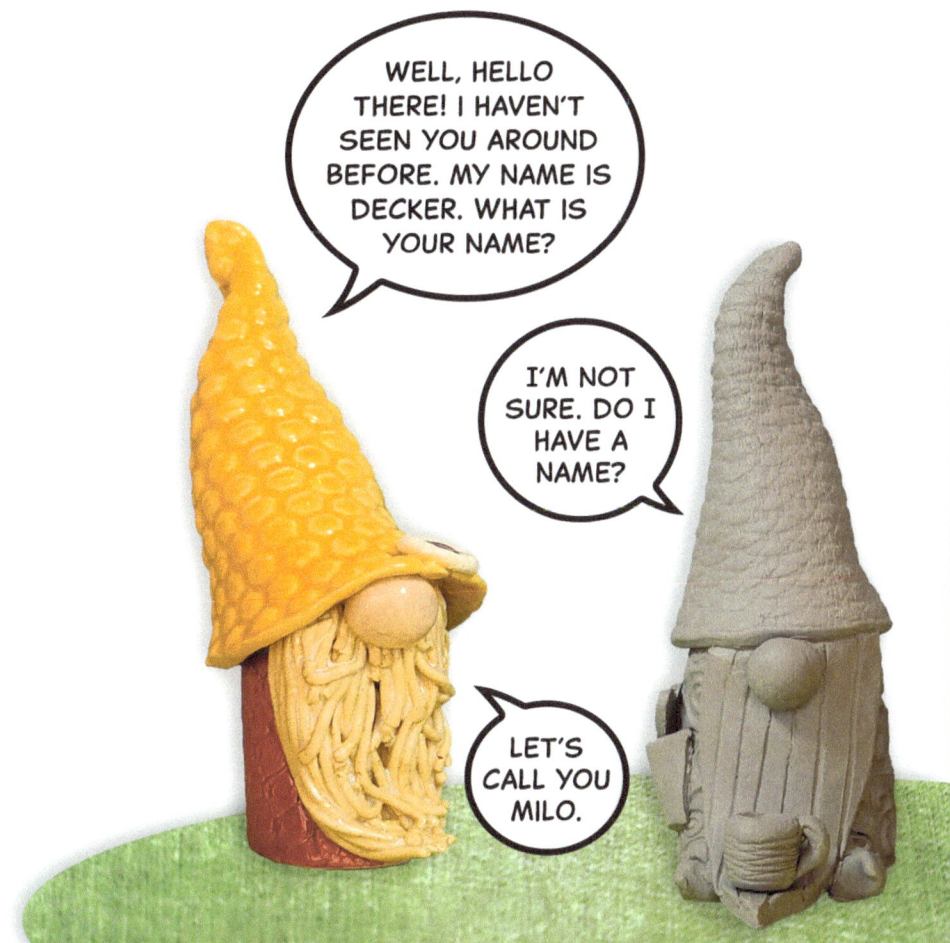

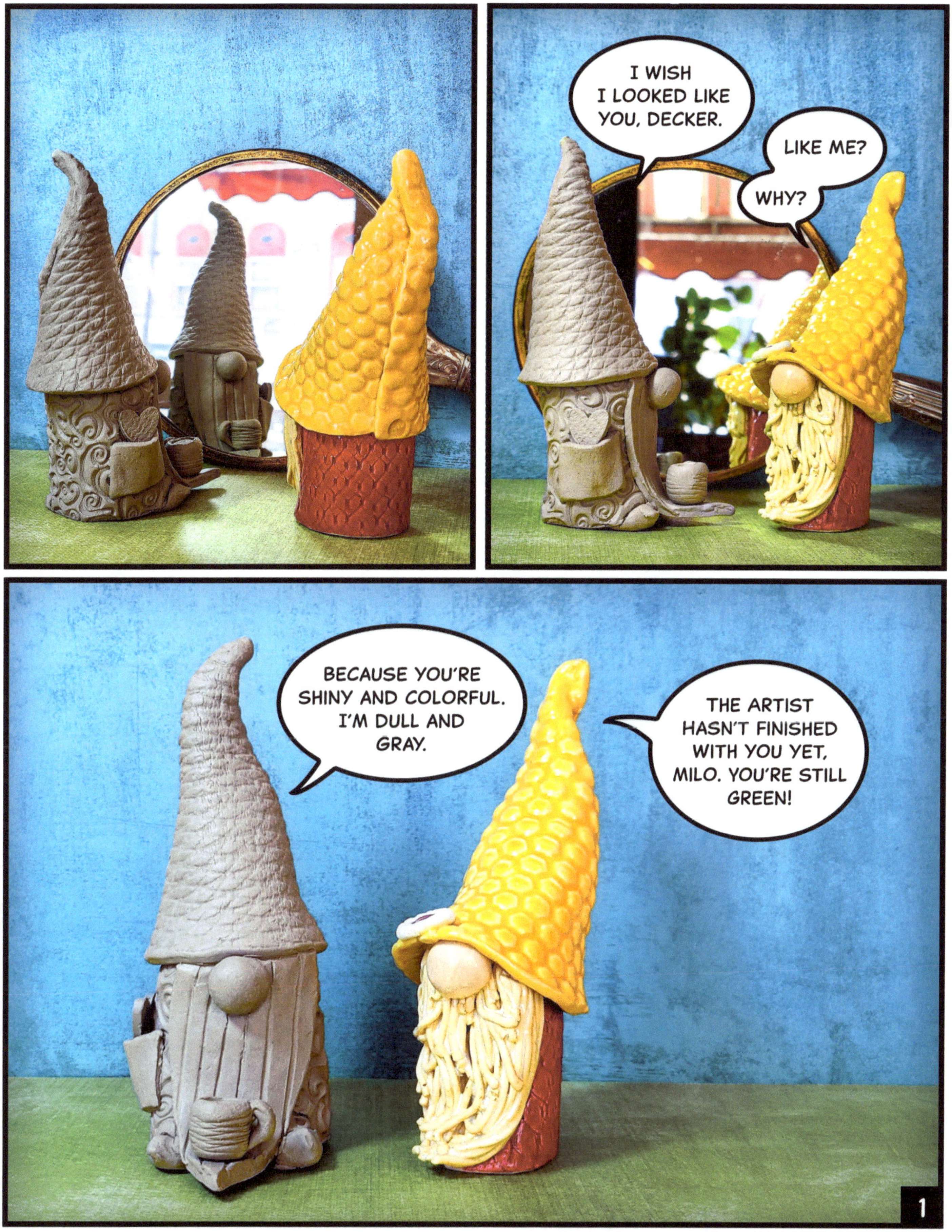

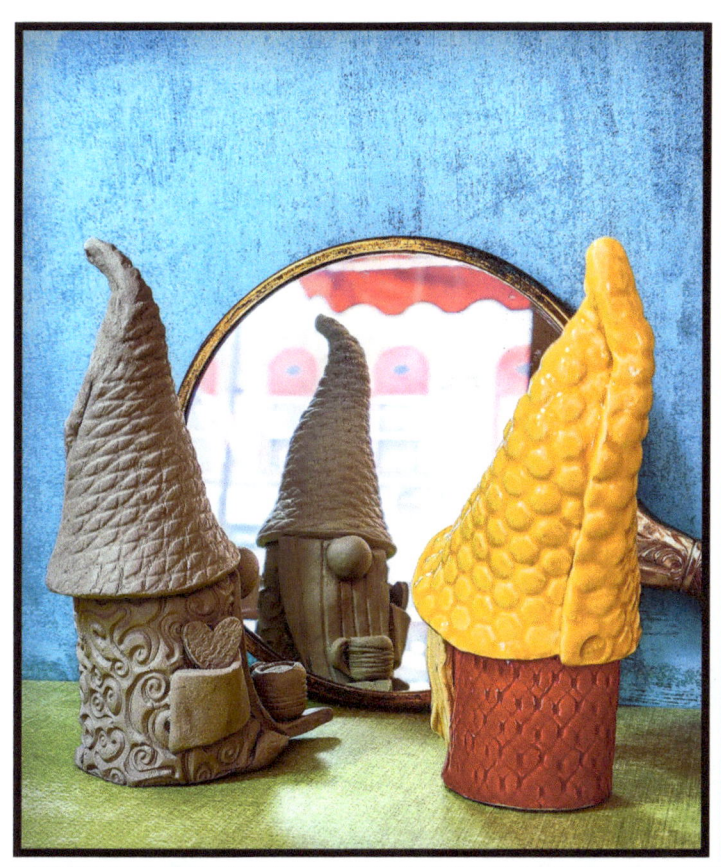
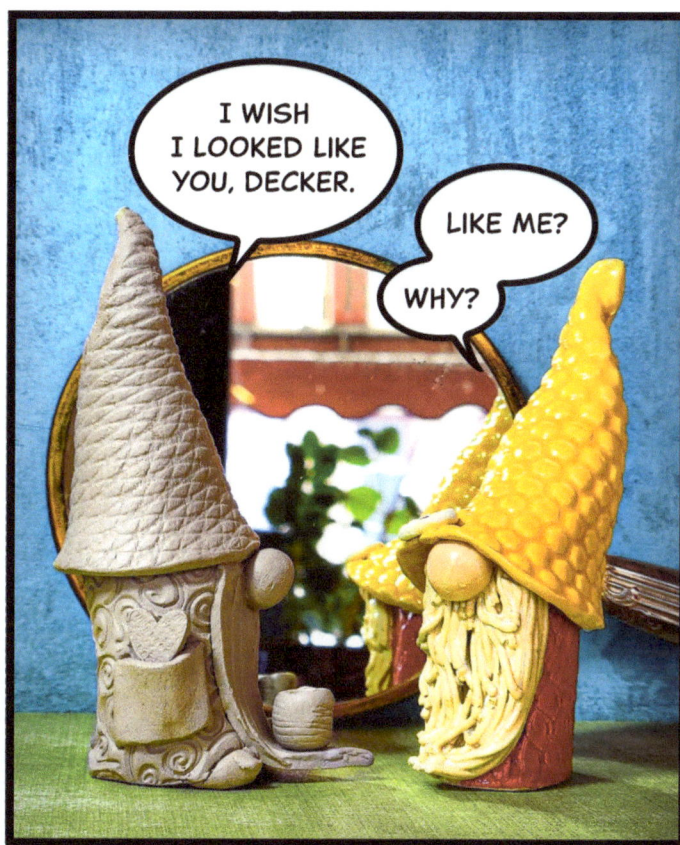

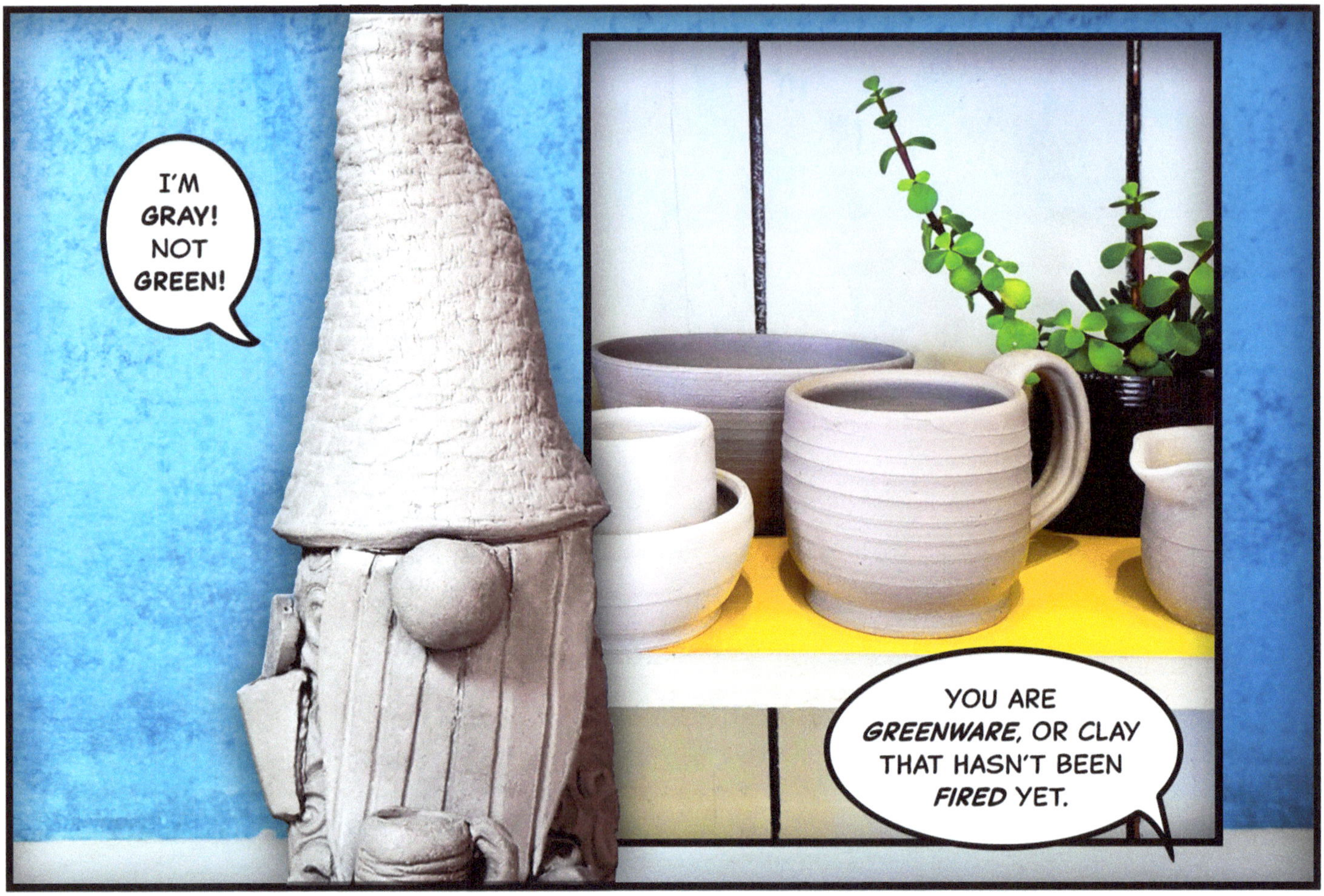

I'M GRAY! NOT GREEN!

YOU ARE *GREENWARE*, OR CLAY THAT HASN'T BEEN *FIRED* YET.

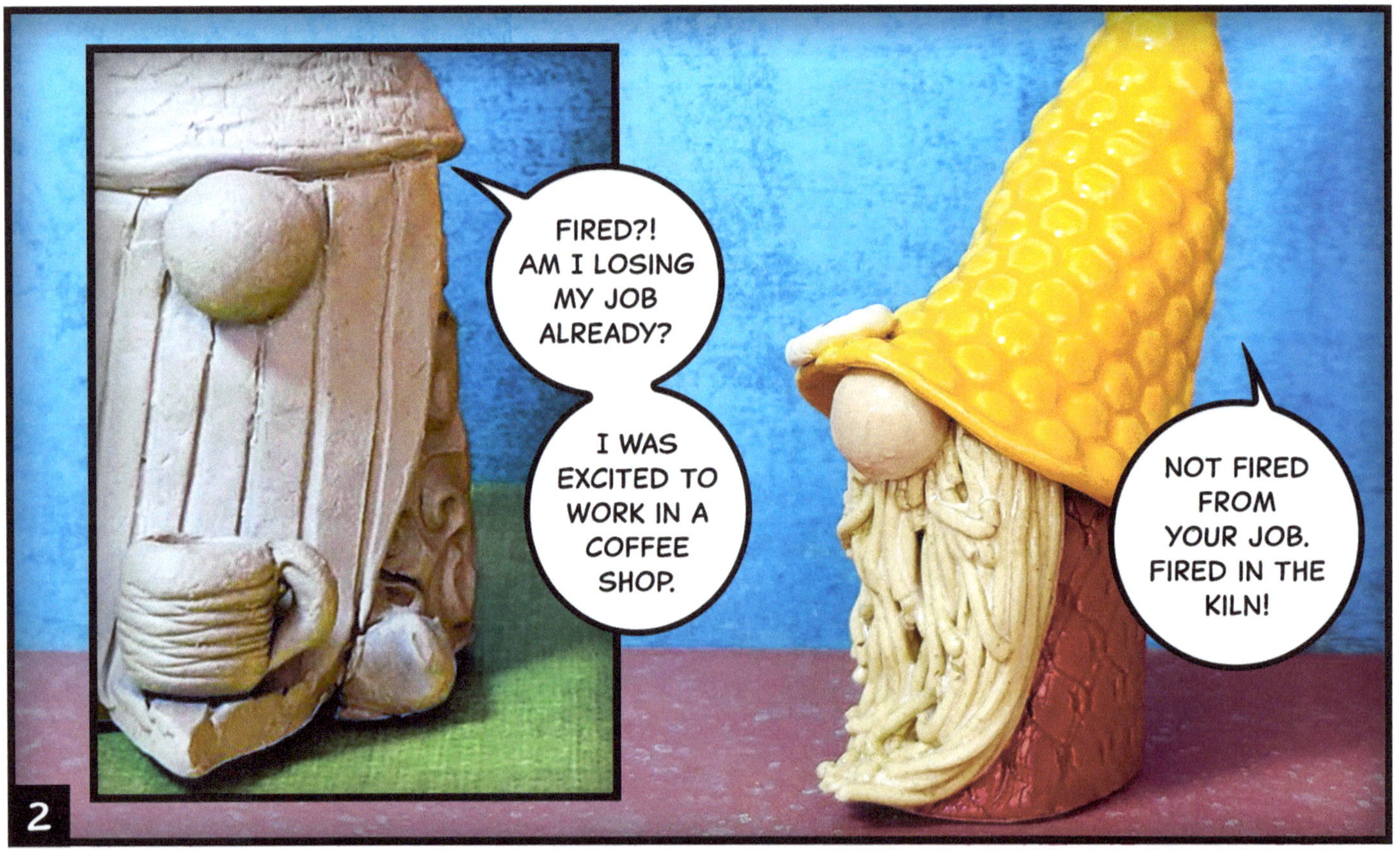

FIRED?! AM I LOSING MY JOB ALREADY?

I WAS EXCITED TO WORK IN A COFFEE SHOP.

NOT FIRED FROM YOUR JOB. FIRED IN THE KILN!

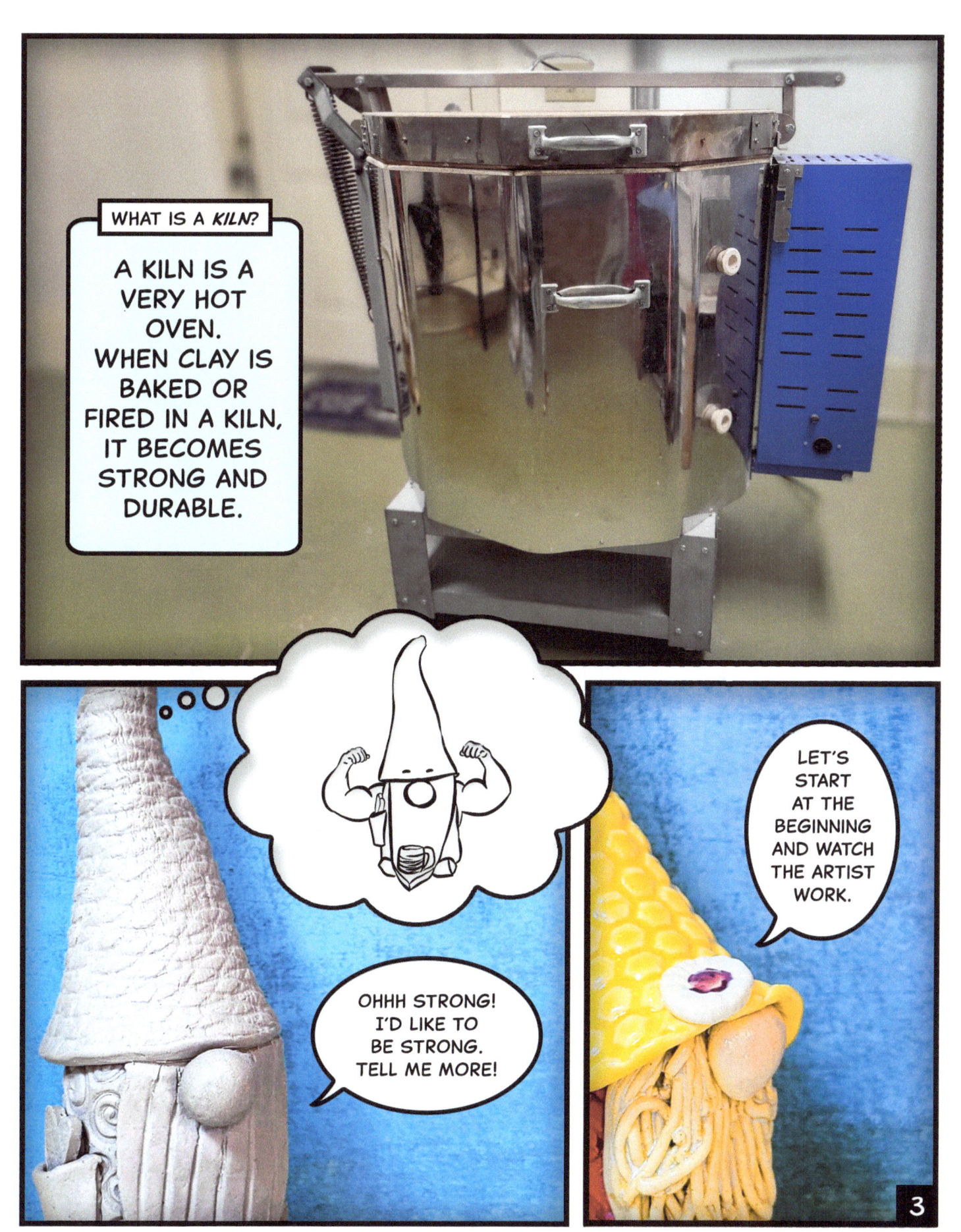

WHAT IS GREENWARE?

THERE ARE MANY DIFFERENT TYPES OF CLAY BUT IT IS ALL CALLED *GREENWARE* IF IT HASN'T BEEN FIRED IN A KILN.

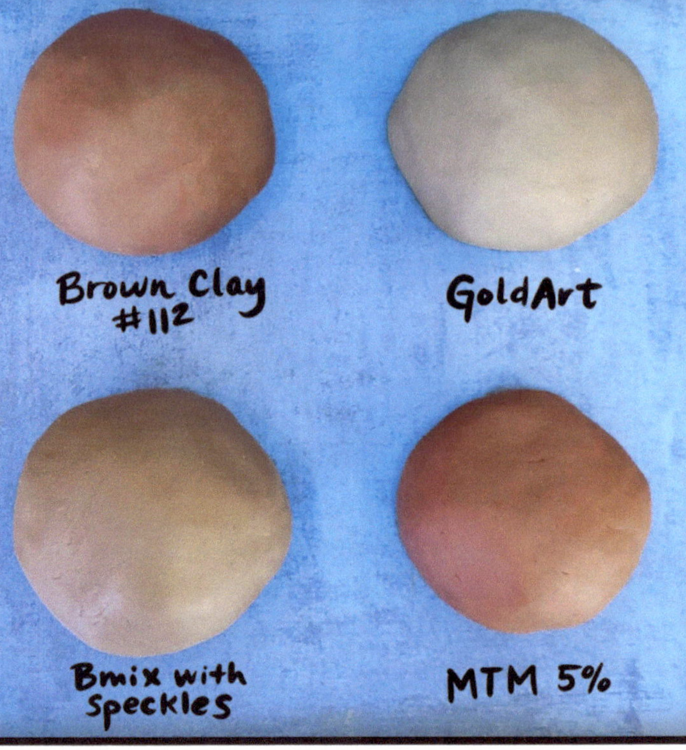

Brown Clay #112

GoldArt

Bmix with Speckles

MTM 5%

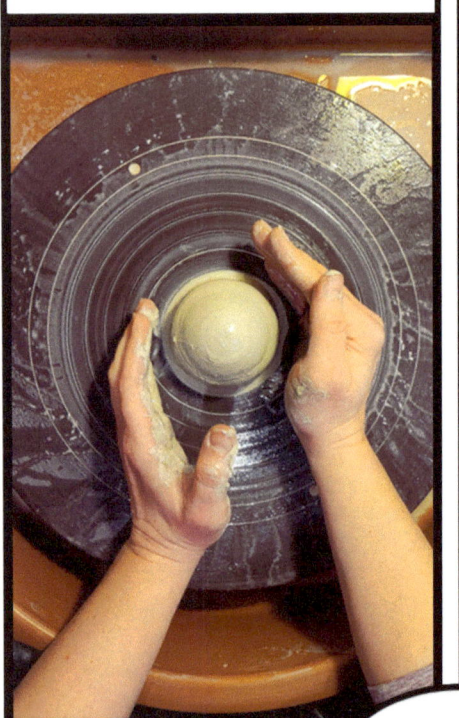

ONE WAY TO CREATE CLAY PIECES IS TO THROW CLAY ON A *POTTER'S WHEEL*.

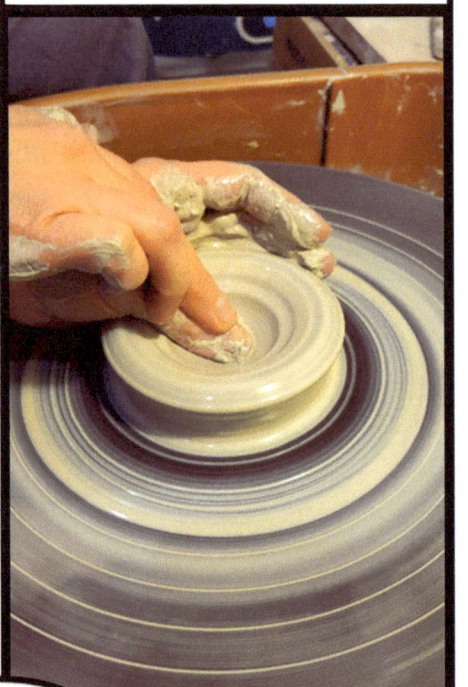

THROWING IS SHAPING CLAY ON A WHEEL AS THE WHEEL TURNS.

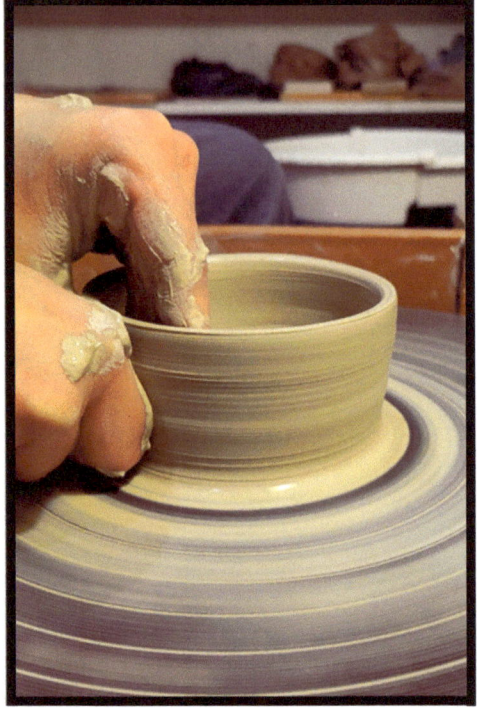

WHEELS ARE OFTEN USED TO MAKE POTS AND BOWLS.

WON'T IT BREAK IF YOU THROW IT?

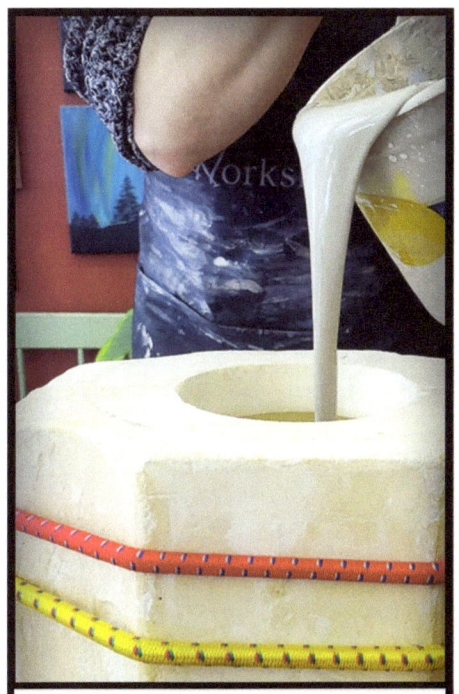

CERAMICS CAN ALSO BE MADE BY *SLIP CASTING* OR POURING LIQUID CLAY INTO *MOLDS*.

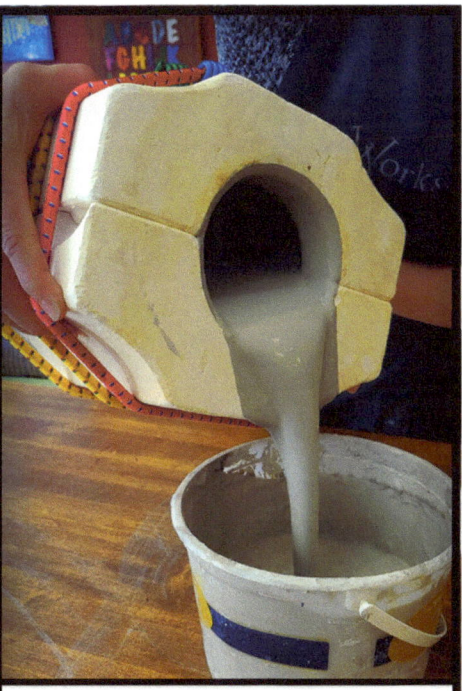

MOLDS ARE USED TO CREATE A LOT OF IDENTICAL PIECES.

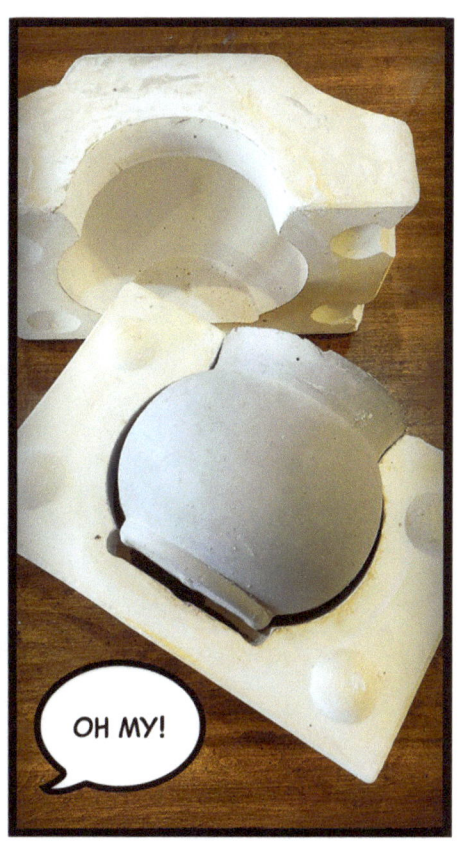

OH MY!

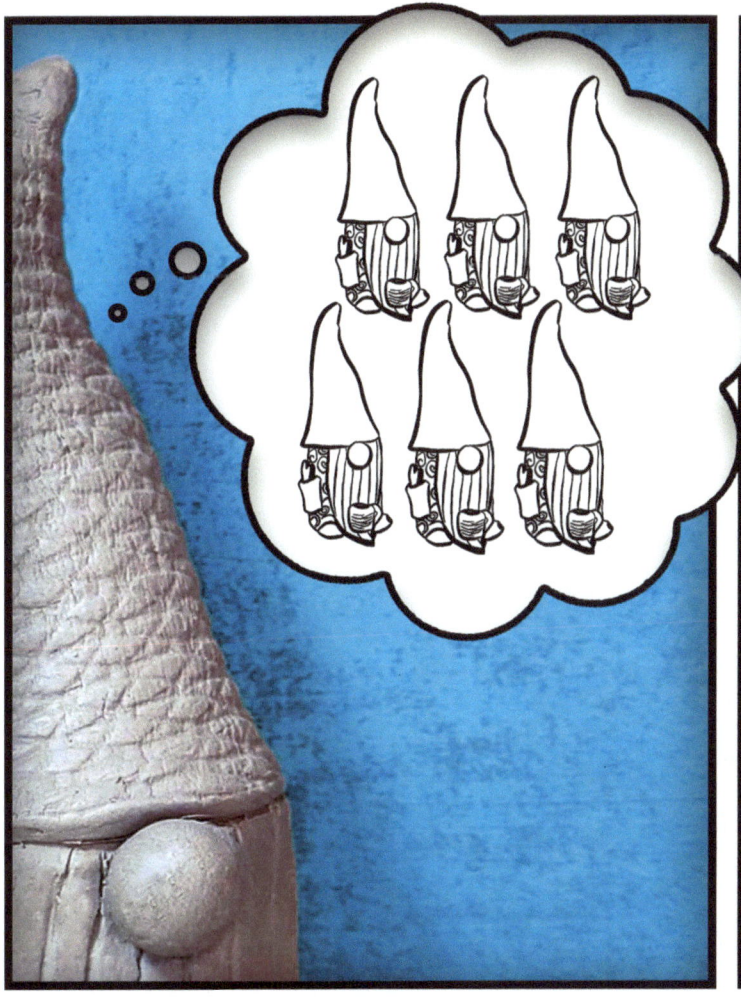

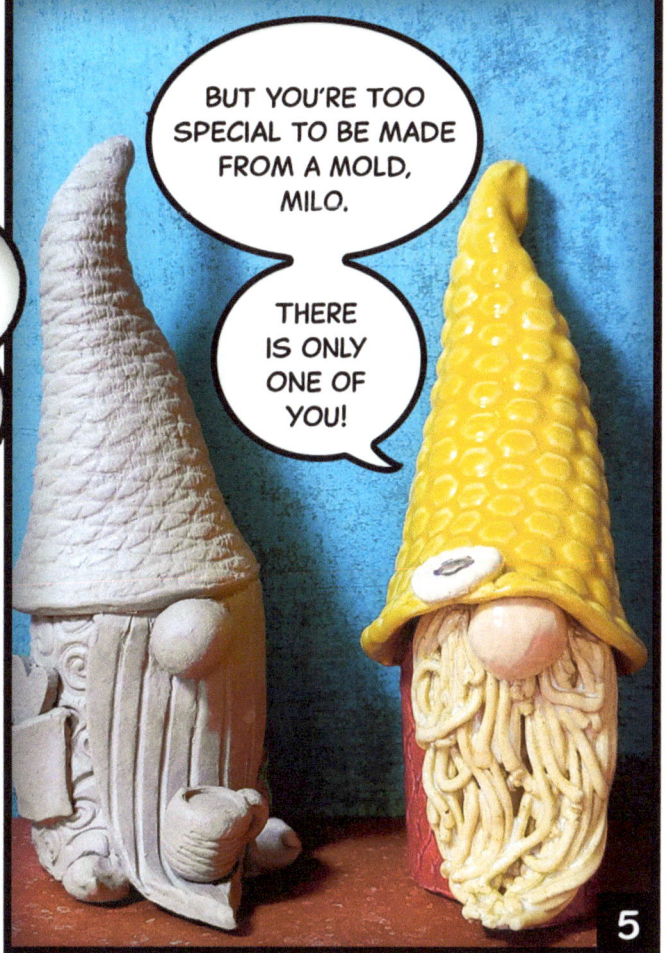

BUT YOU'RE TOO SPECIAL TO BE MADE FROM A MOLD, MILO.

THERE IS ONLY ONE OF YOU!

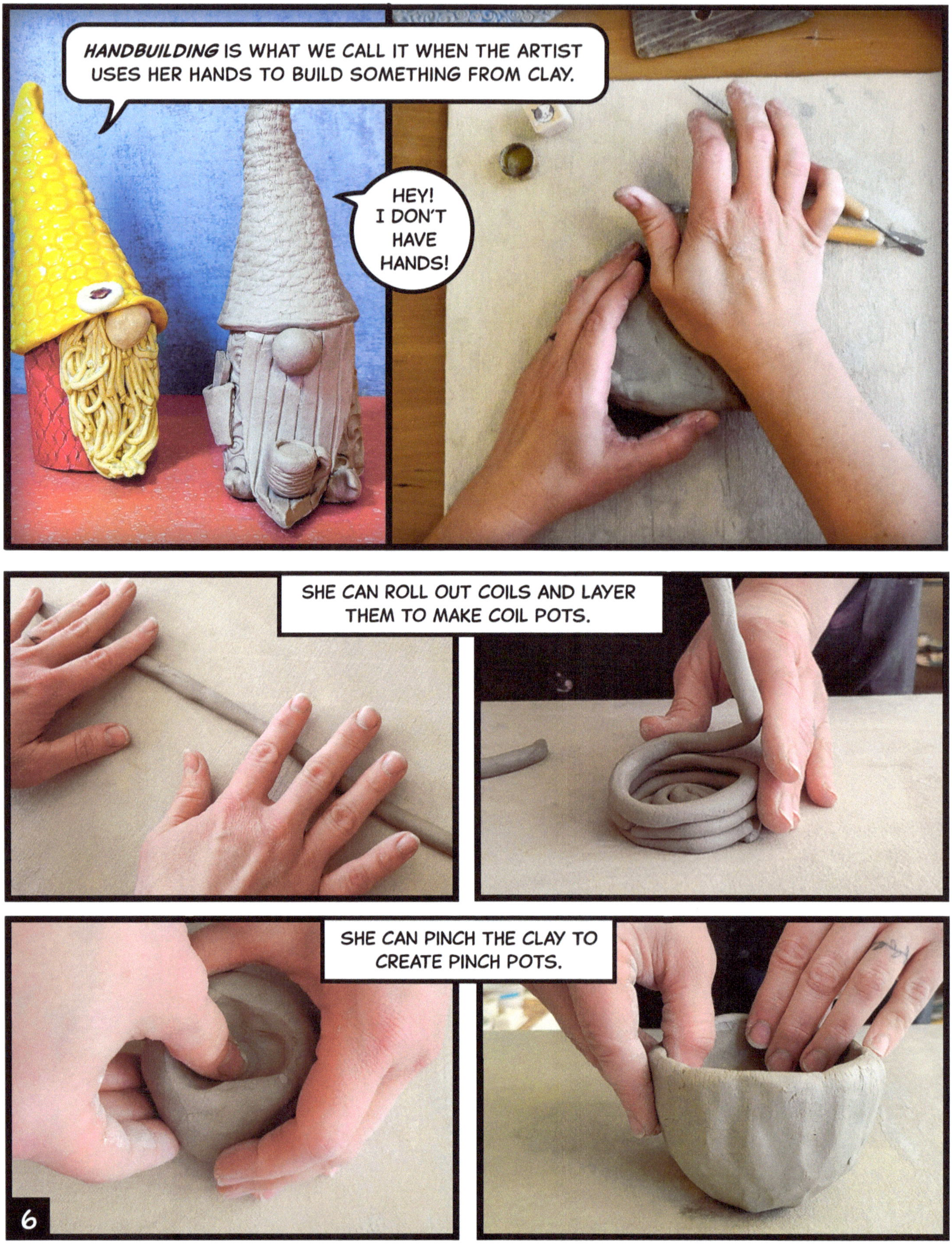

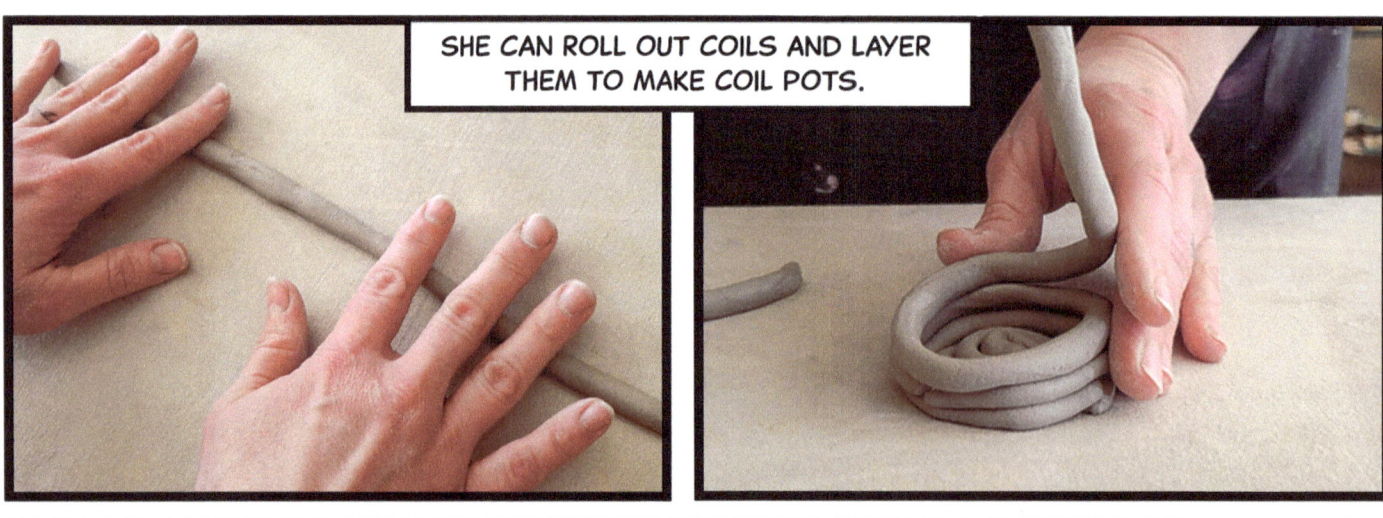

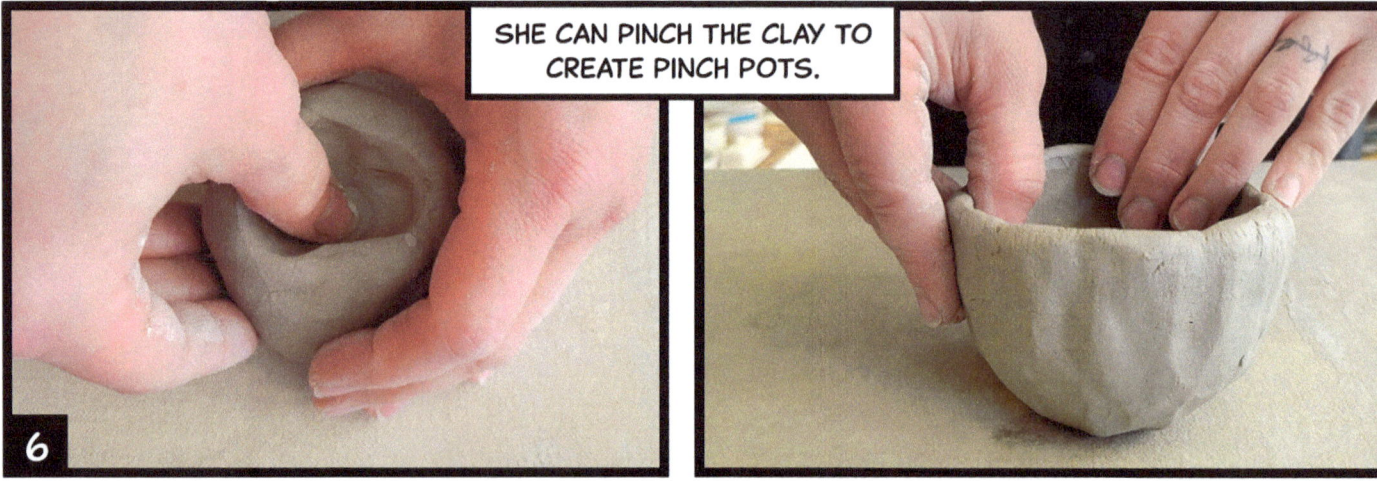

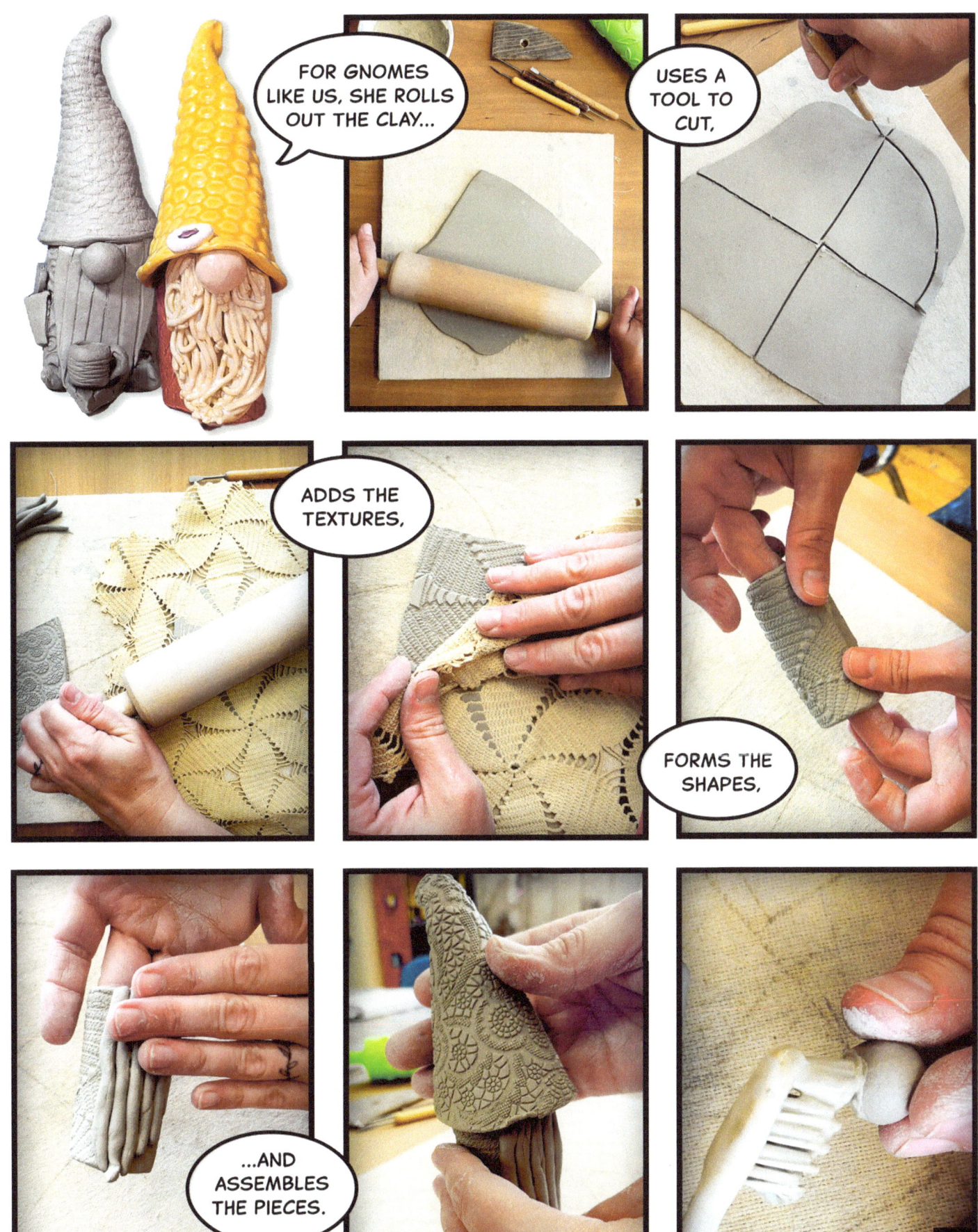

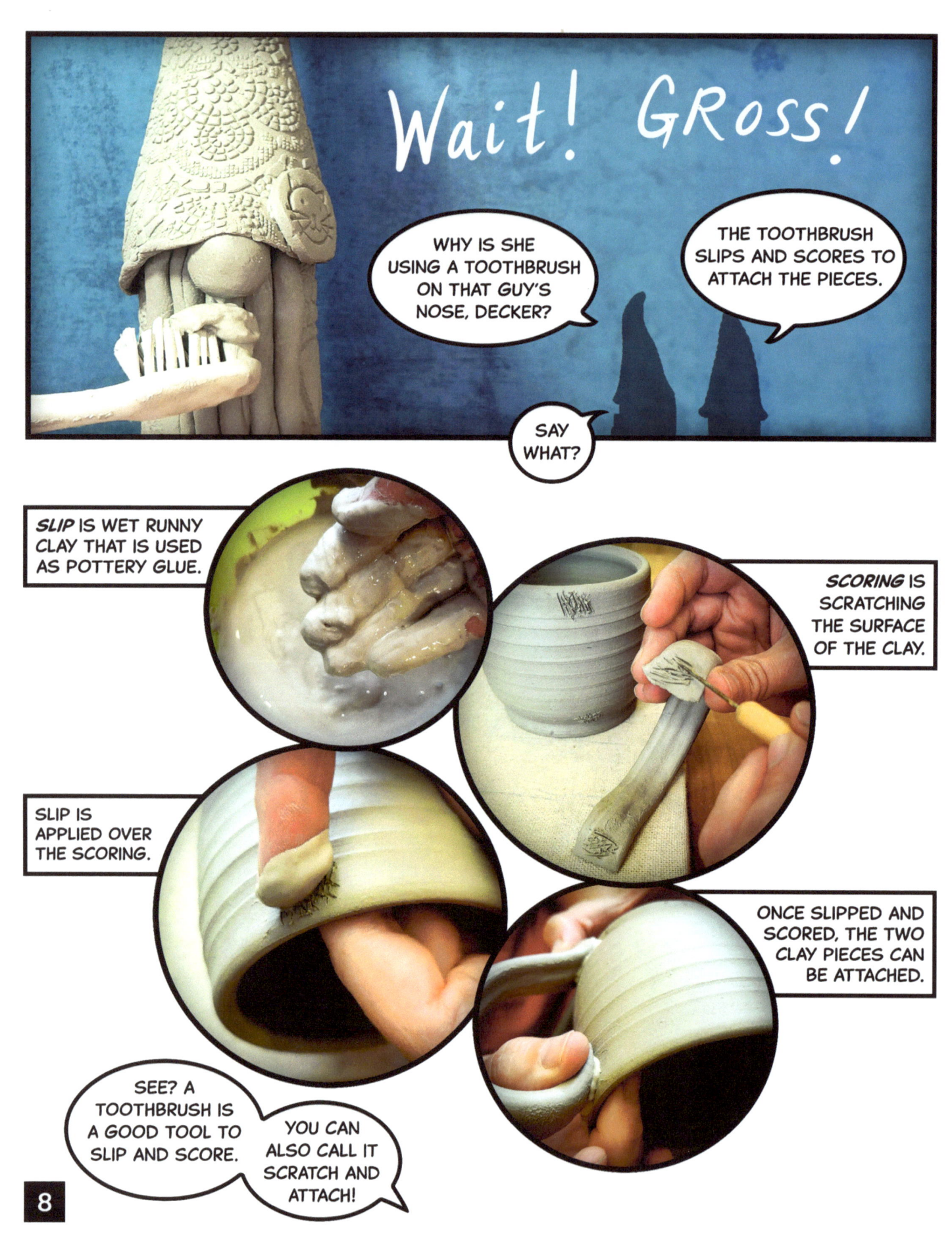

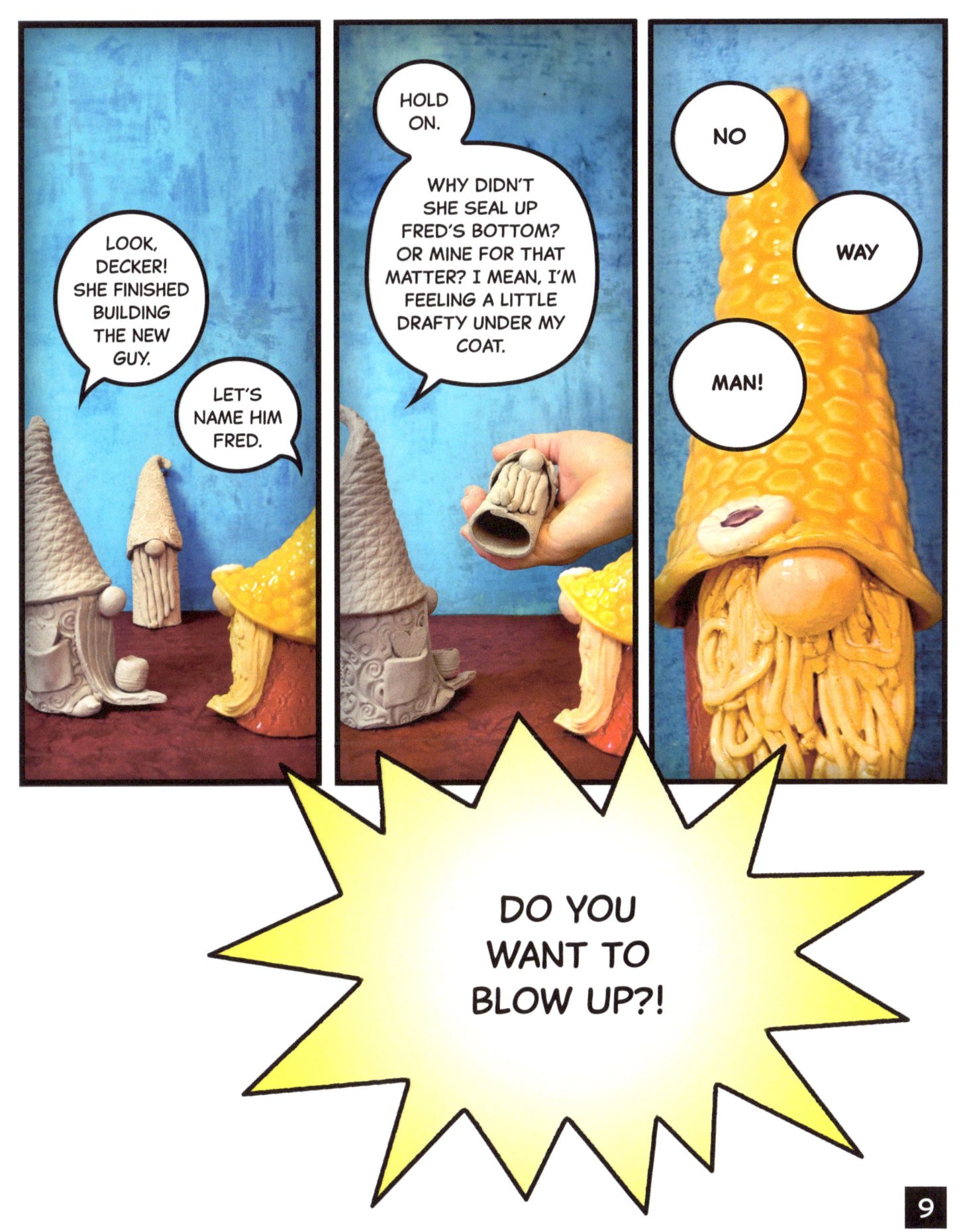

SEALING UP THE BOTTOM WOULD CREATE AN AIR POCKET. MOISTURE IN AIR POCKETS IS DANGEROUS. THE TINIEST AMOUNT OF MOISTURE CAN...

EXPAND

AND EXPAND UNTIL...

BOOM!

OH, AND BYE-BYE FRED.

AND BYE-BYE TO WHATEVER IS NEXT TO FRED IN THE KILN.

WAYS TO PREVENT CERAMICS FROM EXPLODING IN THE KILN:

- CREATE PIECES THAT ARE NOT TOO THICK (LESS THAN AN INCH)
- AVOID BUBBLES OR POCKETS OF AIR
- MAKE SURE PIECES ARE BONE DRY, OR AS DRY AS POSSIBLE
- FIRE SLOWLY OR PREHEAT THE KILN

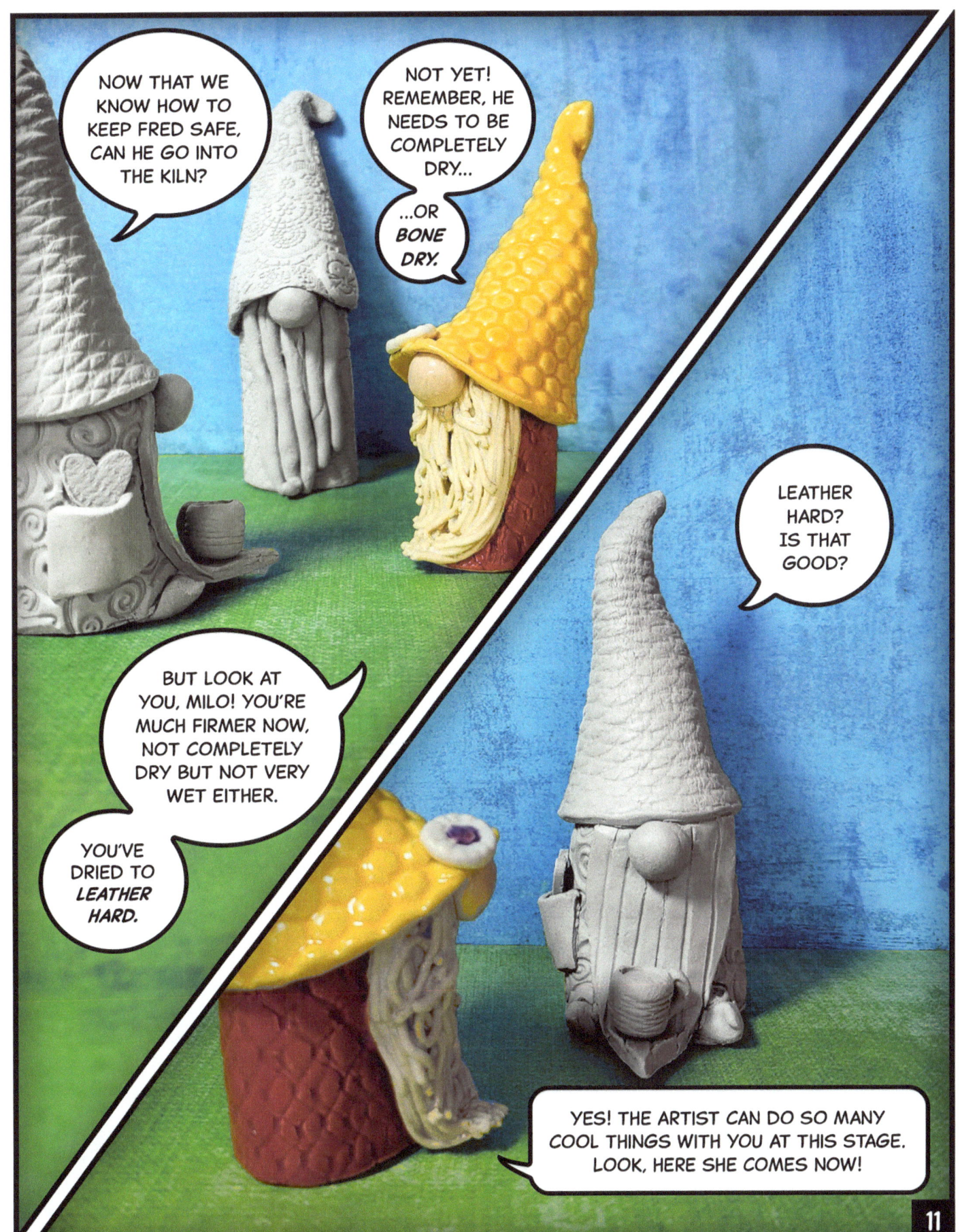

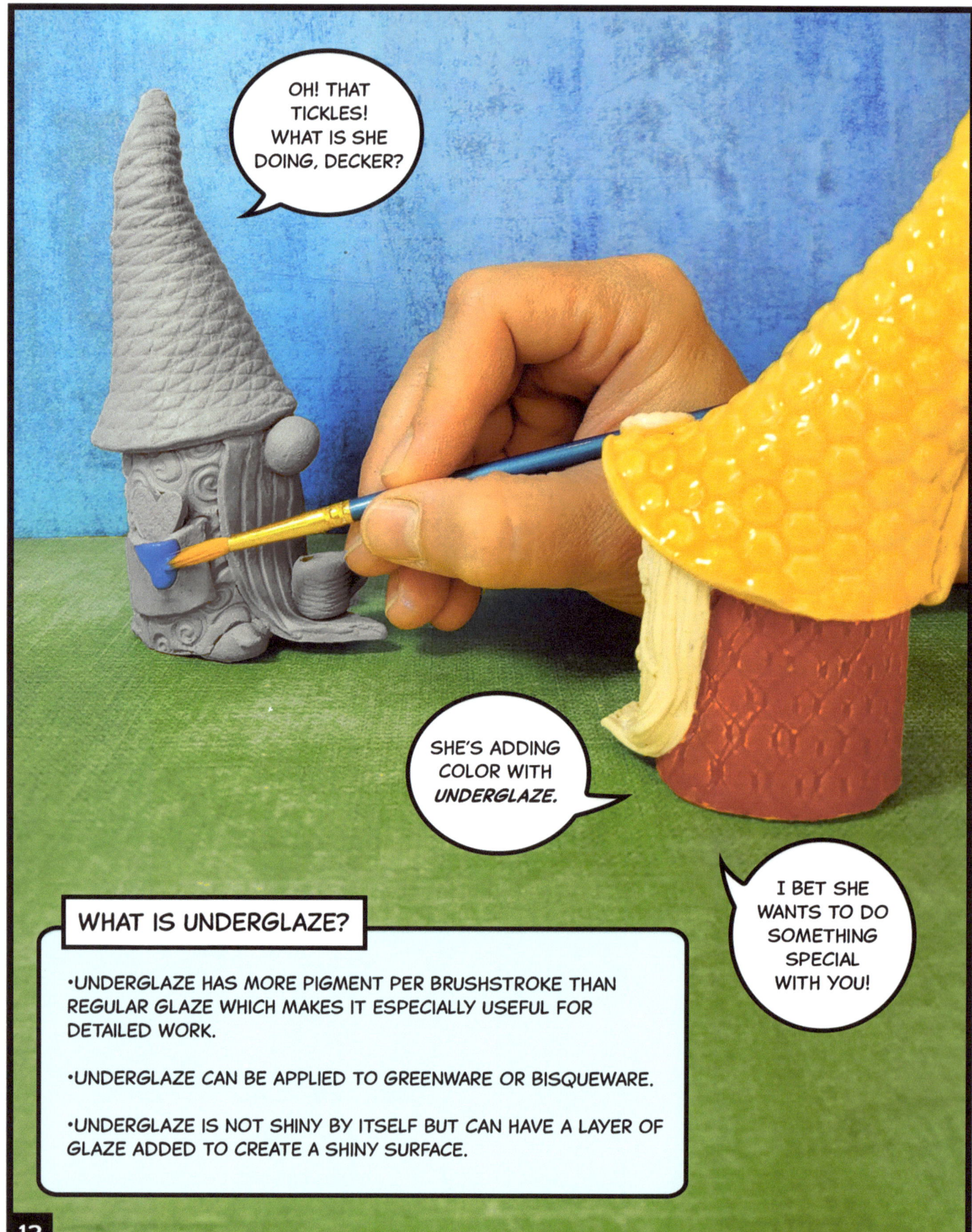

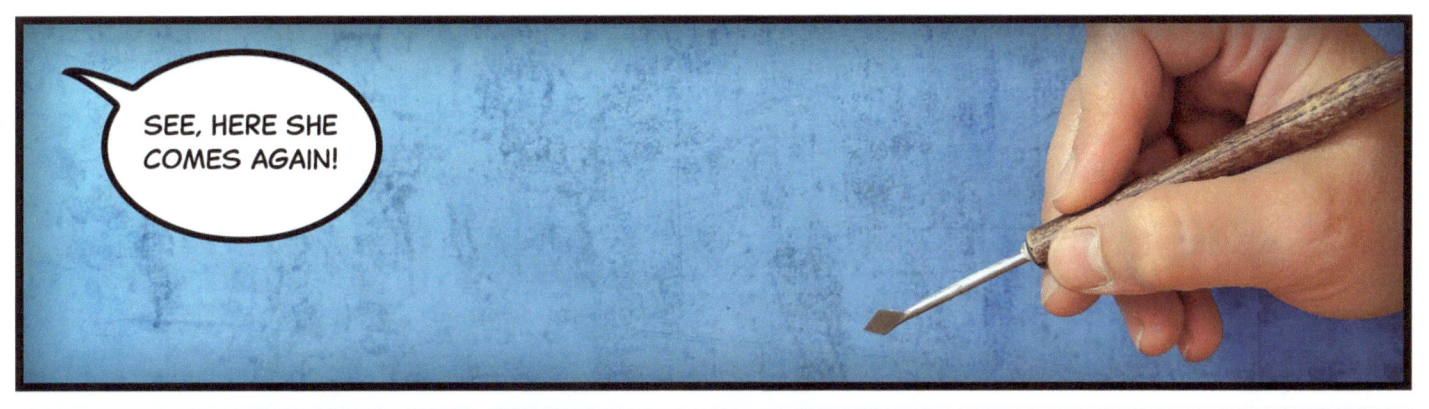
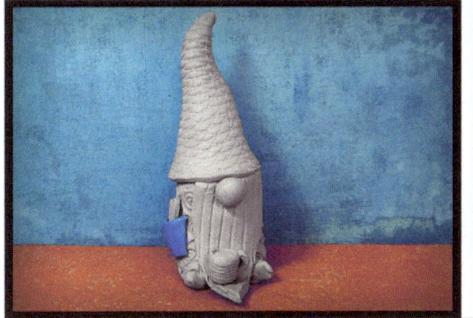
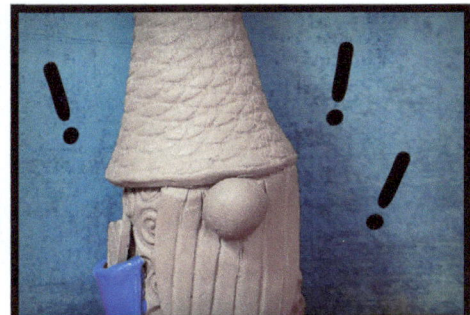
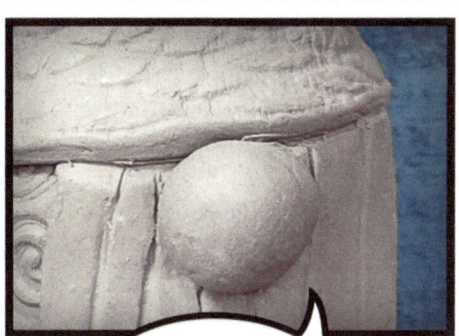
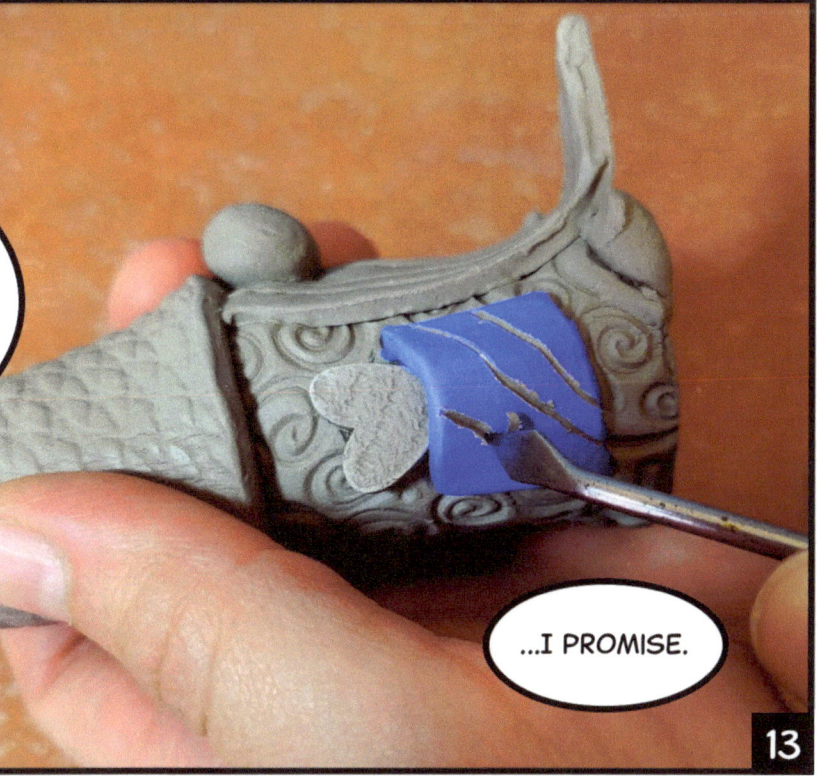

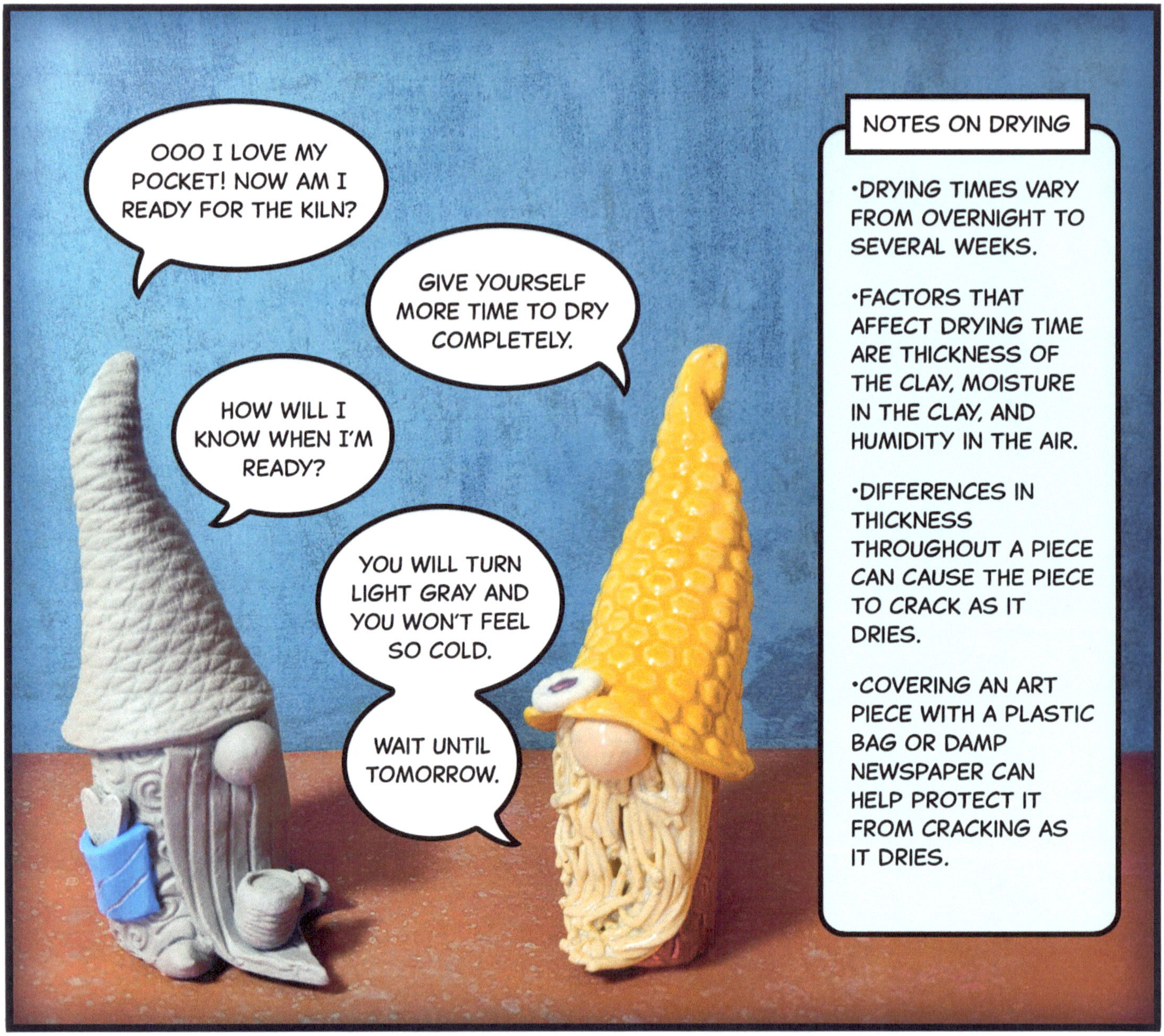

"OOO I LOVE MY POCKET! NOW AM I READY FOR THE KILN?"

"GIVE YOURSELF MORE TIME TO DRY COMPLETELY."

"HOW WILL I KNOW WHEN I'M READY?"

"YOU WILL TURN LIGHT GRAY AND YOU WON'T FEEL SO COLD."

"WAIT UNTIL TOMORROW."

NOTES ON DRYING

- DRYING TIMES VARY FROM OVERNIGHT TO SEVERAL WEEKS.
- FACTORS THAT AFFECT DRYING TIME ARE THICKNESS OF THE CLAY, MOISTURE IN THE CLAY, AND HUMIDITY IN THE AIR.
- DIFFERENCES IN THICKNESS THROUGHOUT A PIECE CAN CAUSE THE PIECE TO CRACK AS IT DRIES.
- COVERING AN ART PIECE WITH A PLASTIC BAG OR DAMP NEWSPAPER CAN HELP PROTECT IT FROM CRACKING AS IT DRIES.

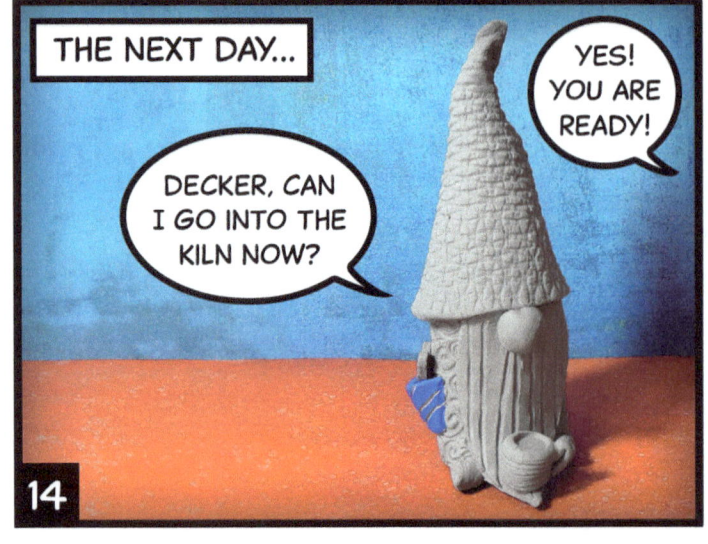

THE NEXT DAY...

"DECKER, CAN I GO INTO THE KILN NOW?"

"YES! YOU ARE READY!"

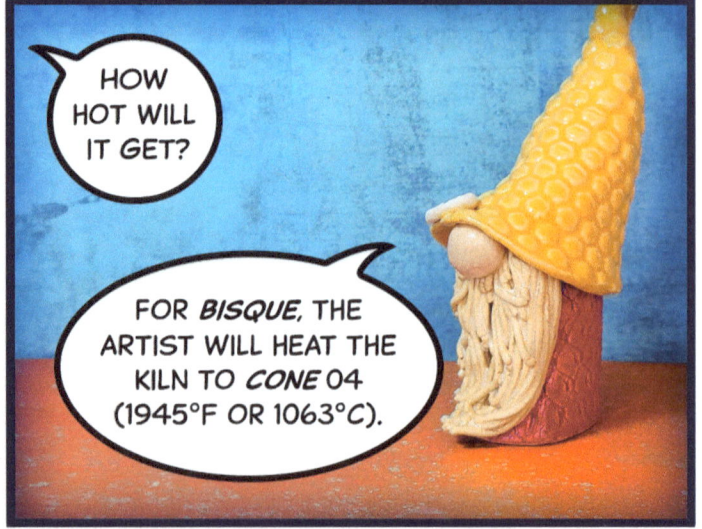

"HOW HOT WILL IT GET?"

"FOR *BISQUE*, THE ARTIST WILL HEAT THE KILN TO *CONE* 04 (1945°F OR 1063°C)."

WHAT IS *BISQUE*?

Bisque or bisqueware: Ceramics that have been fired for the very first time without glaze.

- fires at CONE 04
- takes 8-9 hours to fire
- takes 12 hours to cool

WHAT ARE *CONES*?

CONES ARE PYRAMIDS OF CERAMIC MATERIAL THAT HELP GAUGE IF A KILN HAS HEATED TO A HOT ENOUGH TEMPERATURE OVER THE RIGHT AMOUNT OF TIME TO FIRE THE POTTERY SUFFICIENTLY.

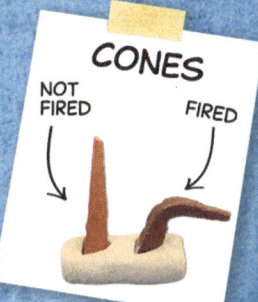

CONES — NOT FIRED / FIRED

CONE CHART*

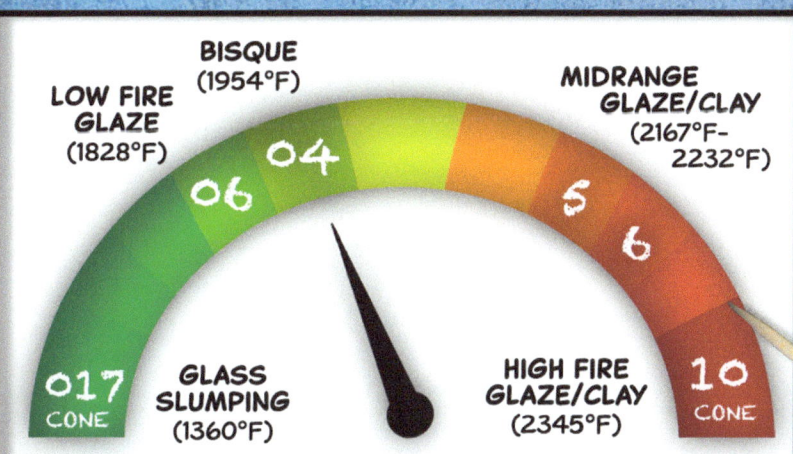

LOW FIRE GLAZE (1828°F)
BISQUE (1954°F)
MIDRANGE GLAZE/CLAY (2167°F-2232°F)
017 CONE
06
04
5
6
GLASS SLUMPING (1360°F)
HIGH FIRE GLAZE/CLAY (2345°F)
10 CONE

THE CONES BEND OVER WHEN THEY REACH THE CORRECT TEMPERATURE/ TIME!

EACH PHYSICAL CONE MATCHES A CORRESPONDING NUMBER ON THE CONE CHART. CONES RANGE FROM THE LOWER TEMP/TIME CONE 022 TO THE HIGHER TEMP/TIME CONE 12.

SOME KILNS RELY ONLY ON PHYSICAL CONES TO DETERMINE IF THE CERAMICS HAVE BEEN FIRED SUFFICIENTLY. OTHER KILNS HAVE AN ELECTRONIC CONTROL PANEL TO HELP ACHIEVE THE CORRECT CONE RATING.

*YOU WILL FIND A MORE COMPLETE CONE CHART IN THE BACK OF THE BOOK

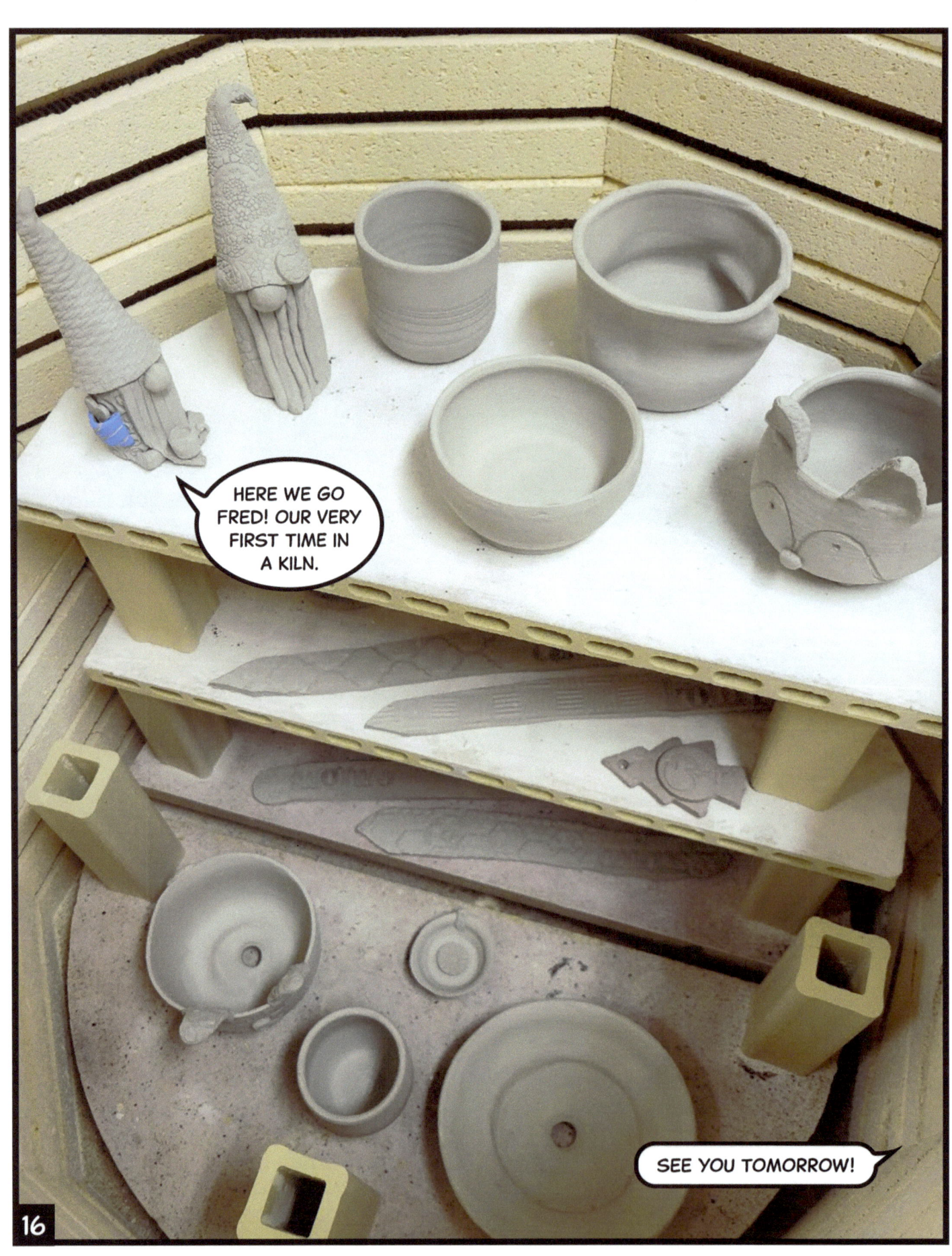

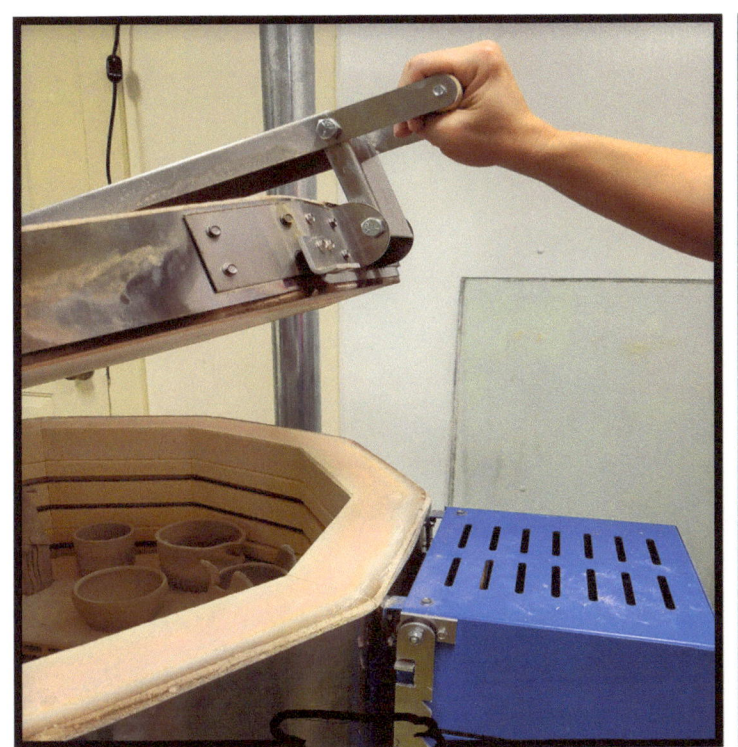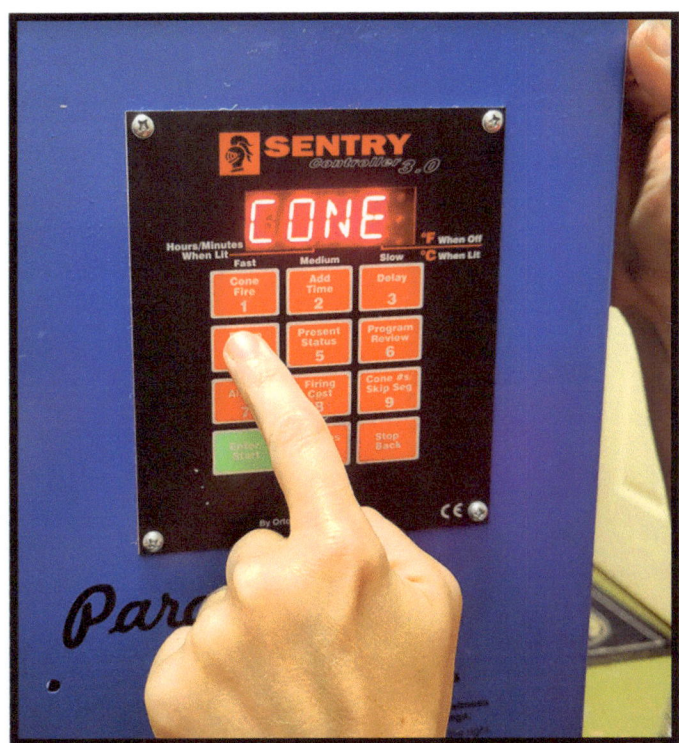

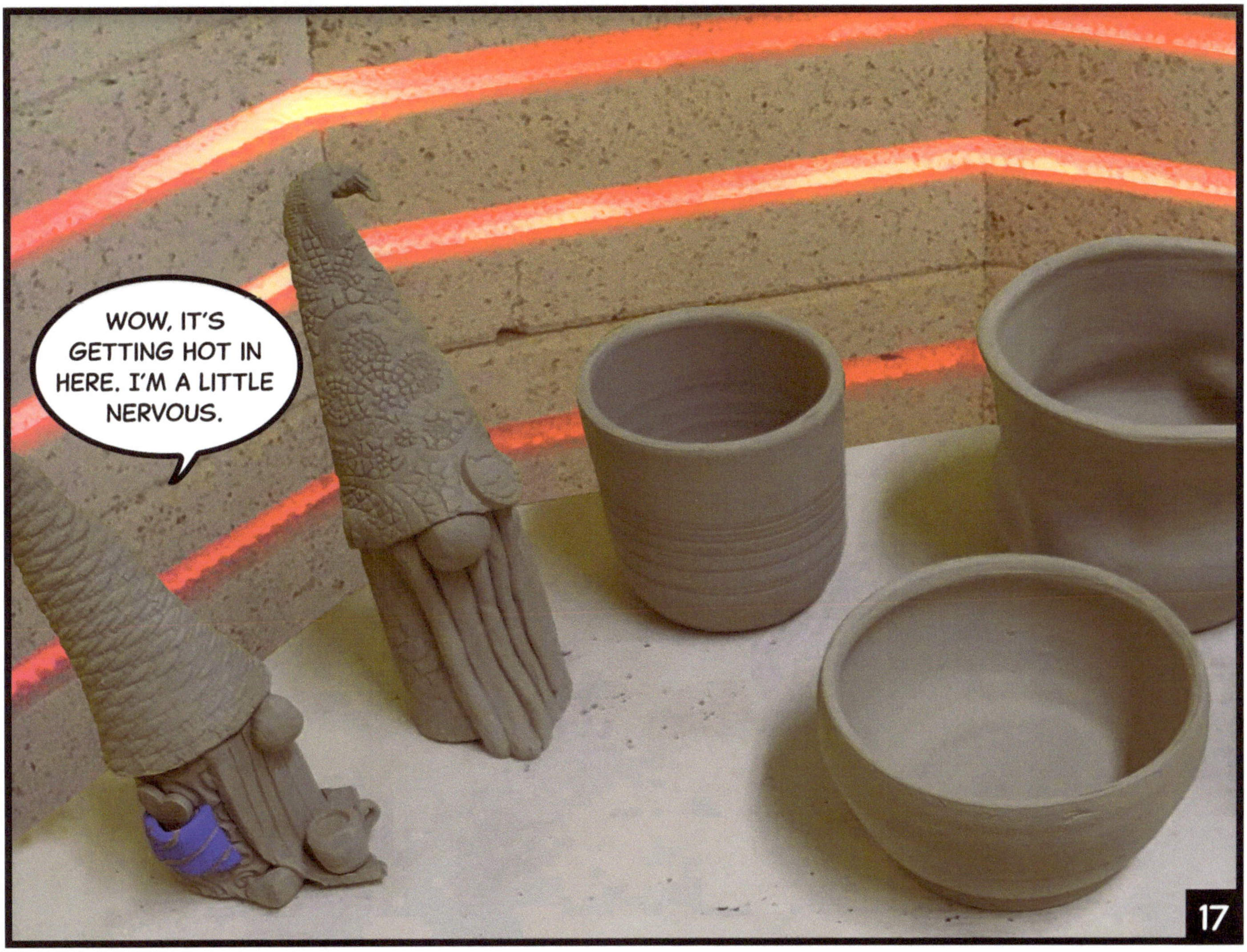

WOW, IT'S GETTING HOT IN HERE. I'M A LITTLE NERVOUS.

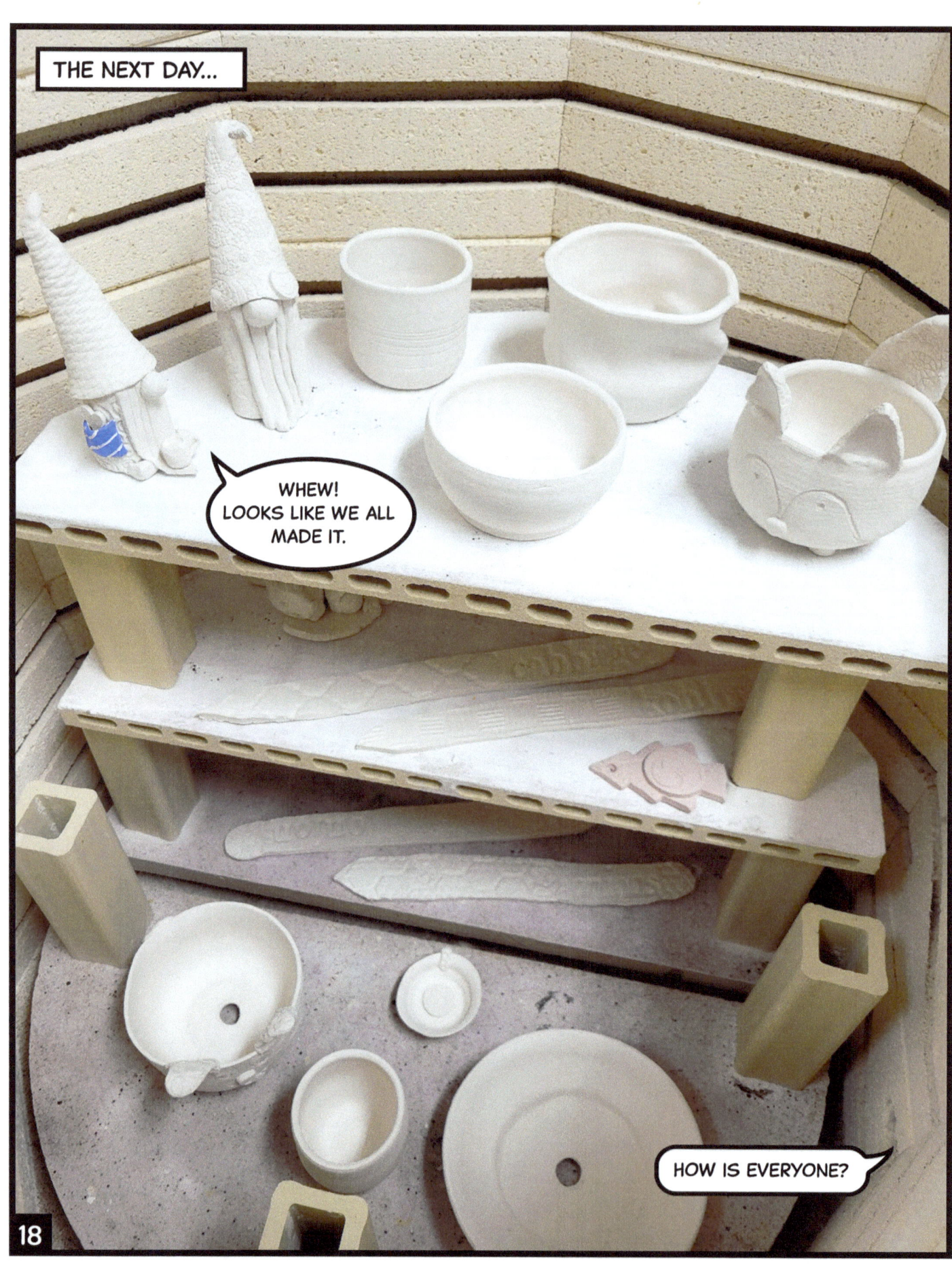

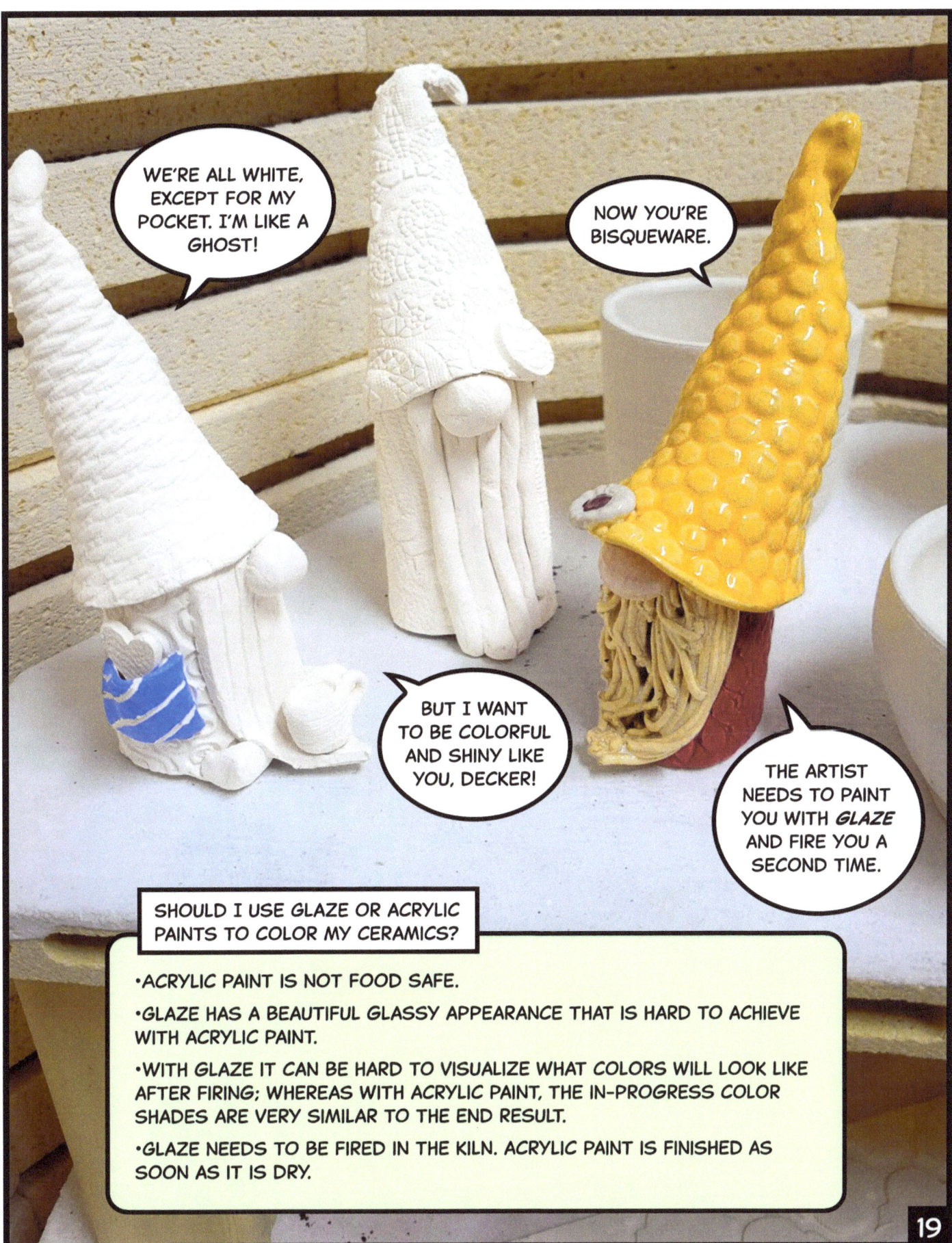

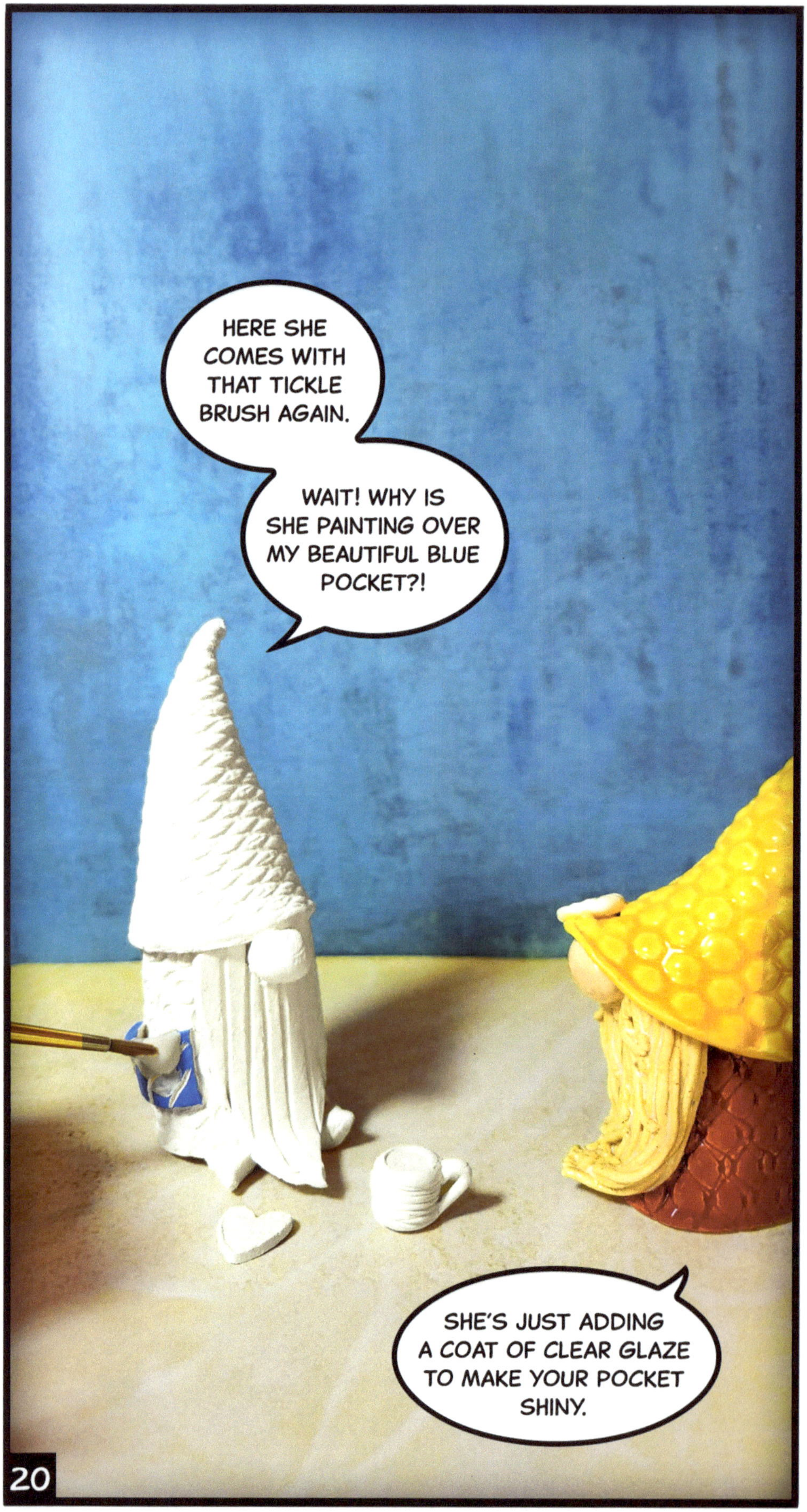

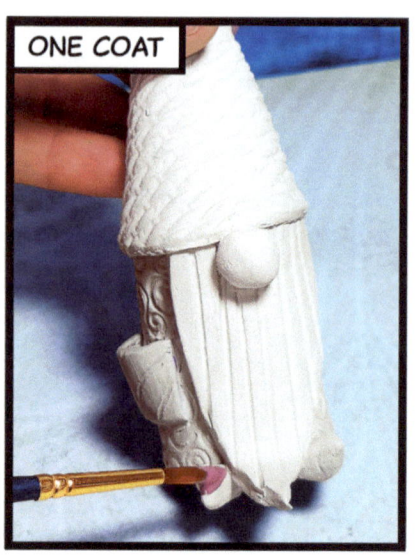

ONE COAT

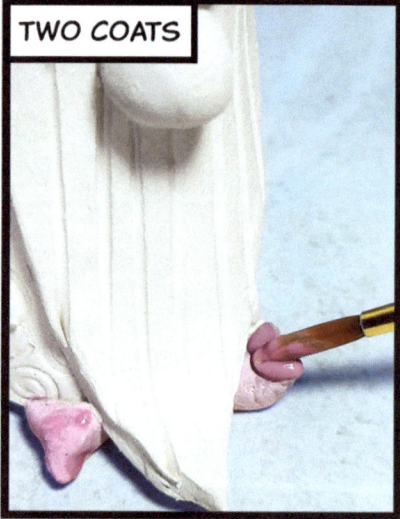

TWO COATS

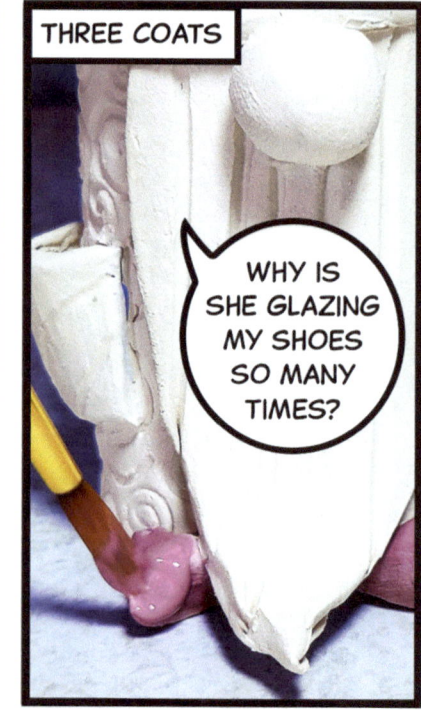

THREE COATS

"HERE SHE COMES WITH THAT TICKLE BRUSH AGAIN."

"WAIT! WHY IS SHE PAINTING OVER MY BEAUTIFUL BLUE POCKET?!"

"SHE'S JUST ADDING A COAT OF CLEAR GLAZE TO MAKE YOUR POCKET SHINY."

"WHY IS SHE GLAZING MY SHOES SO MANY TIMES?"

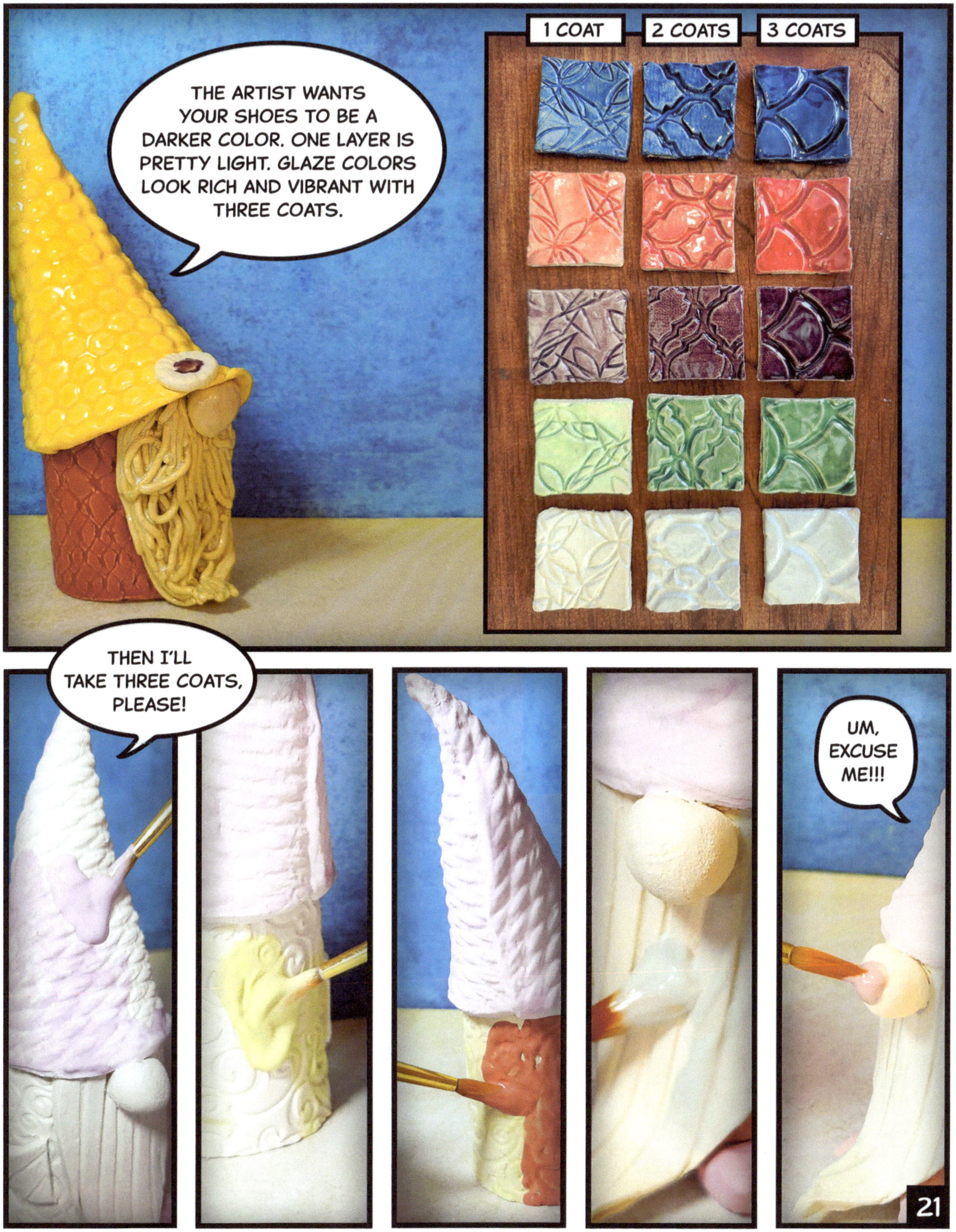

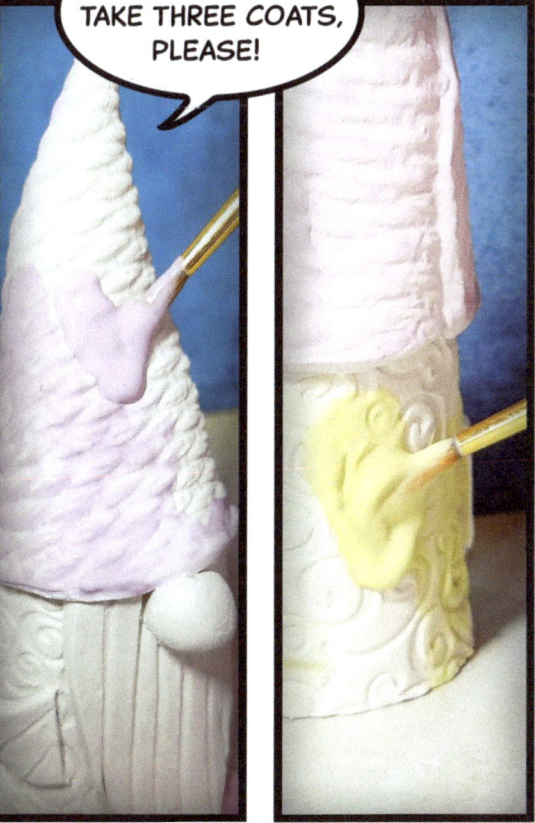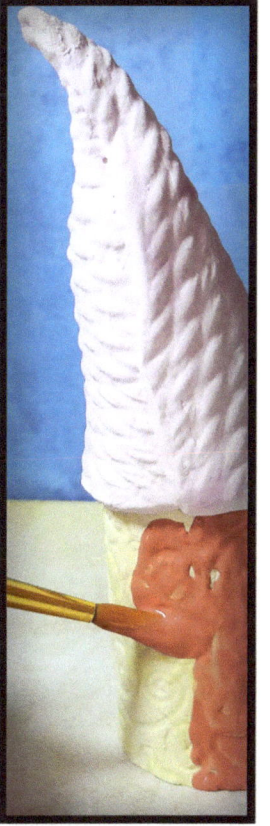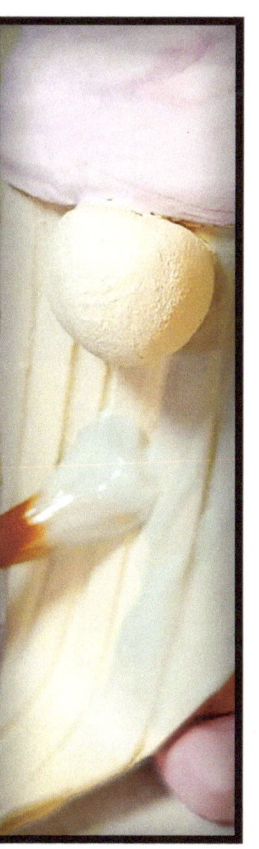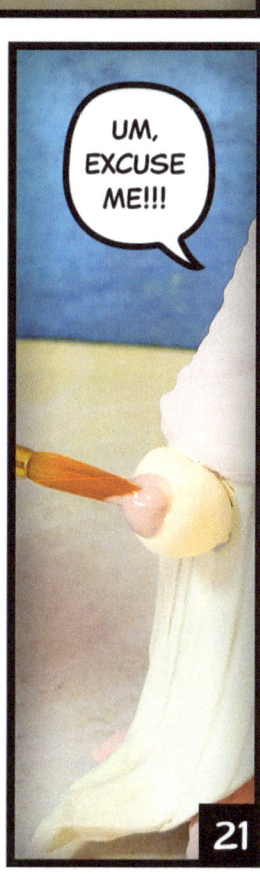

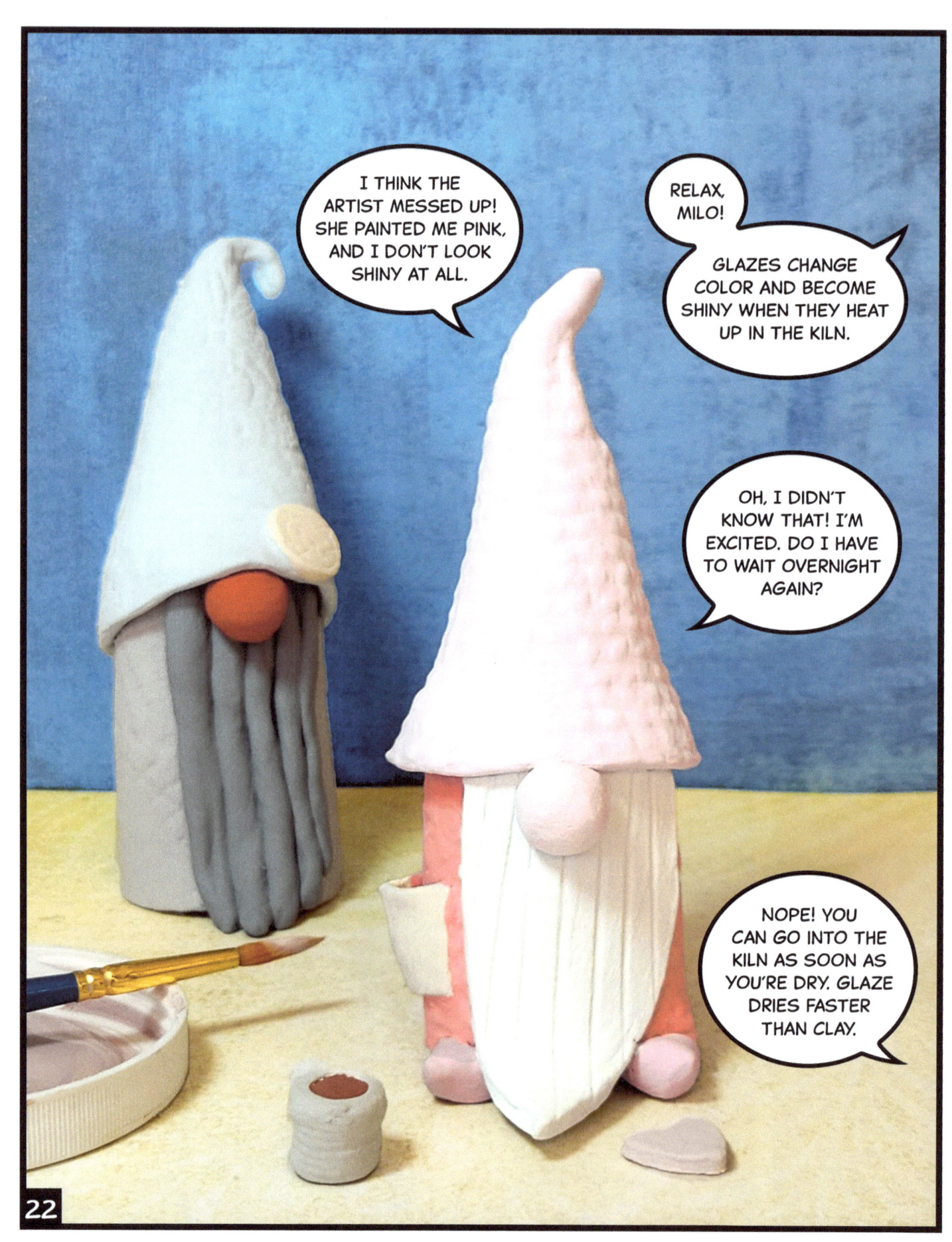

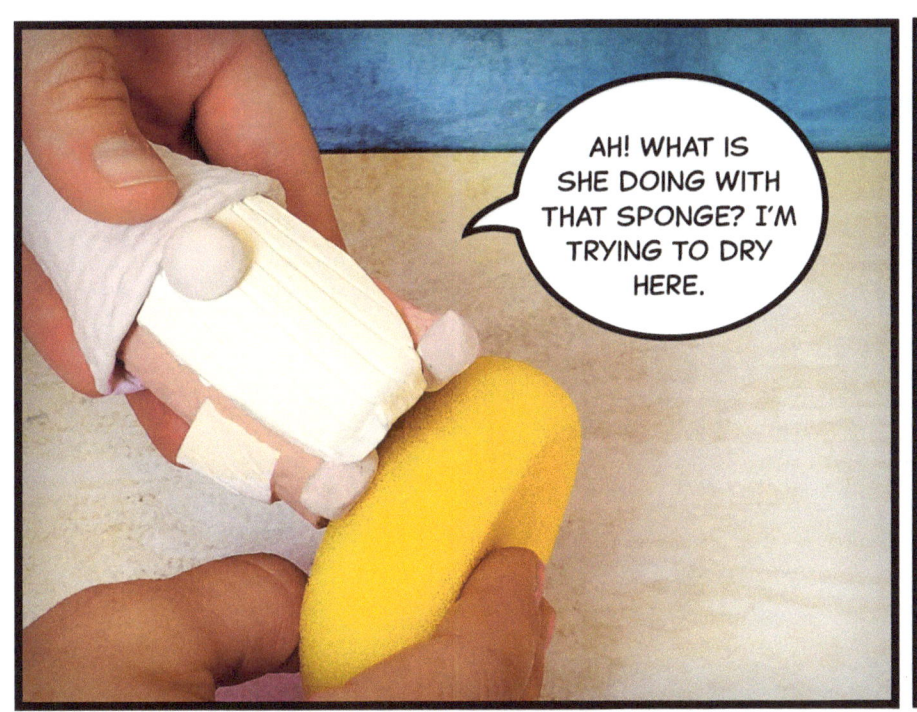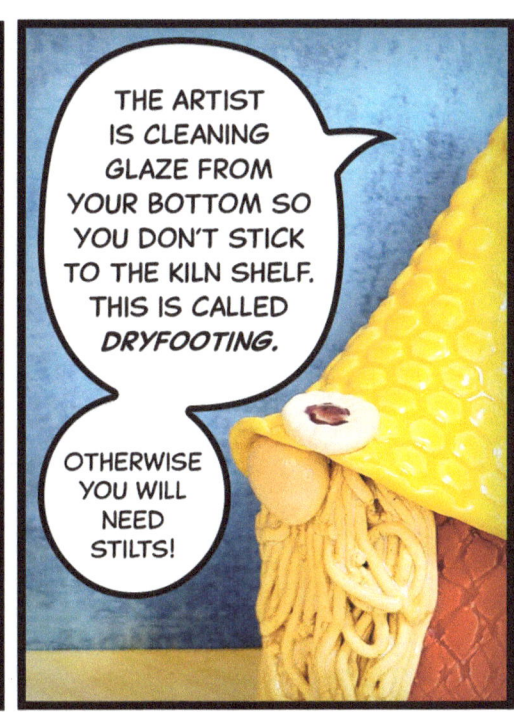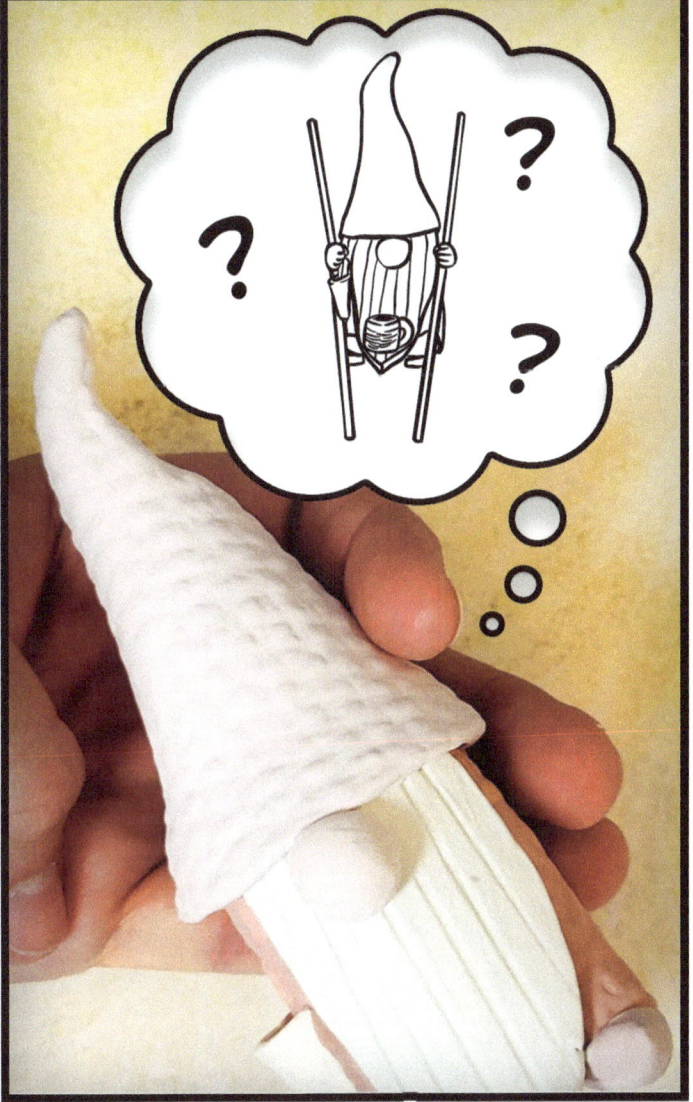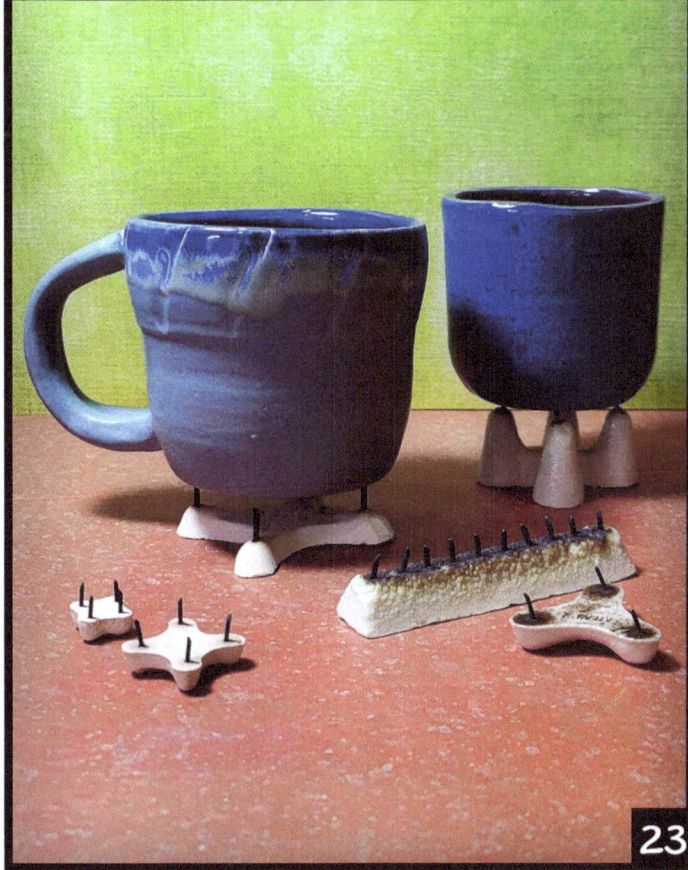

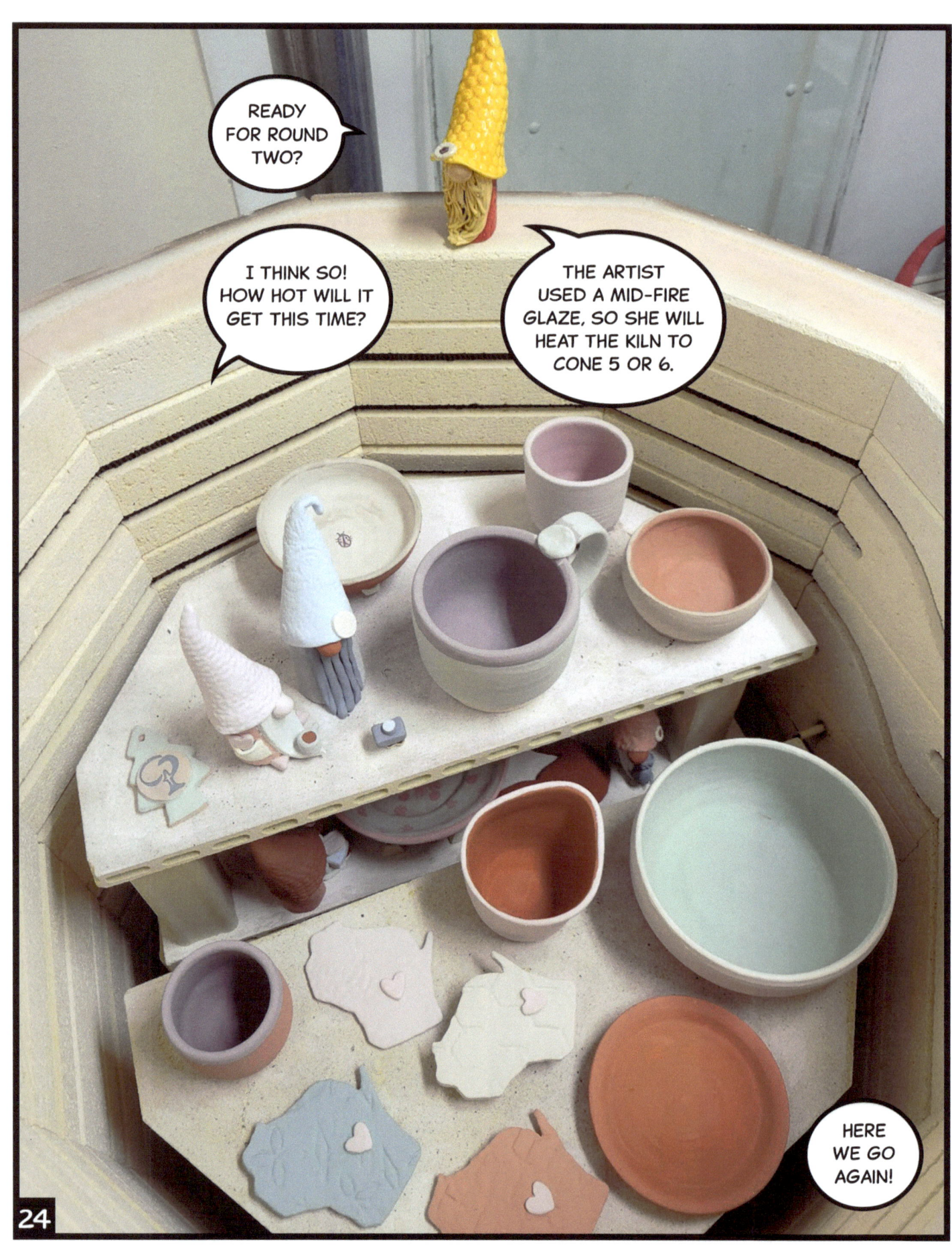

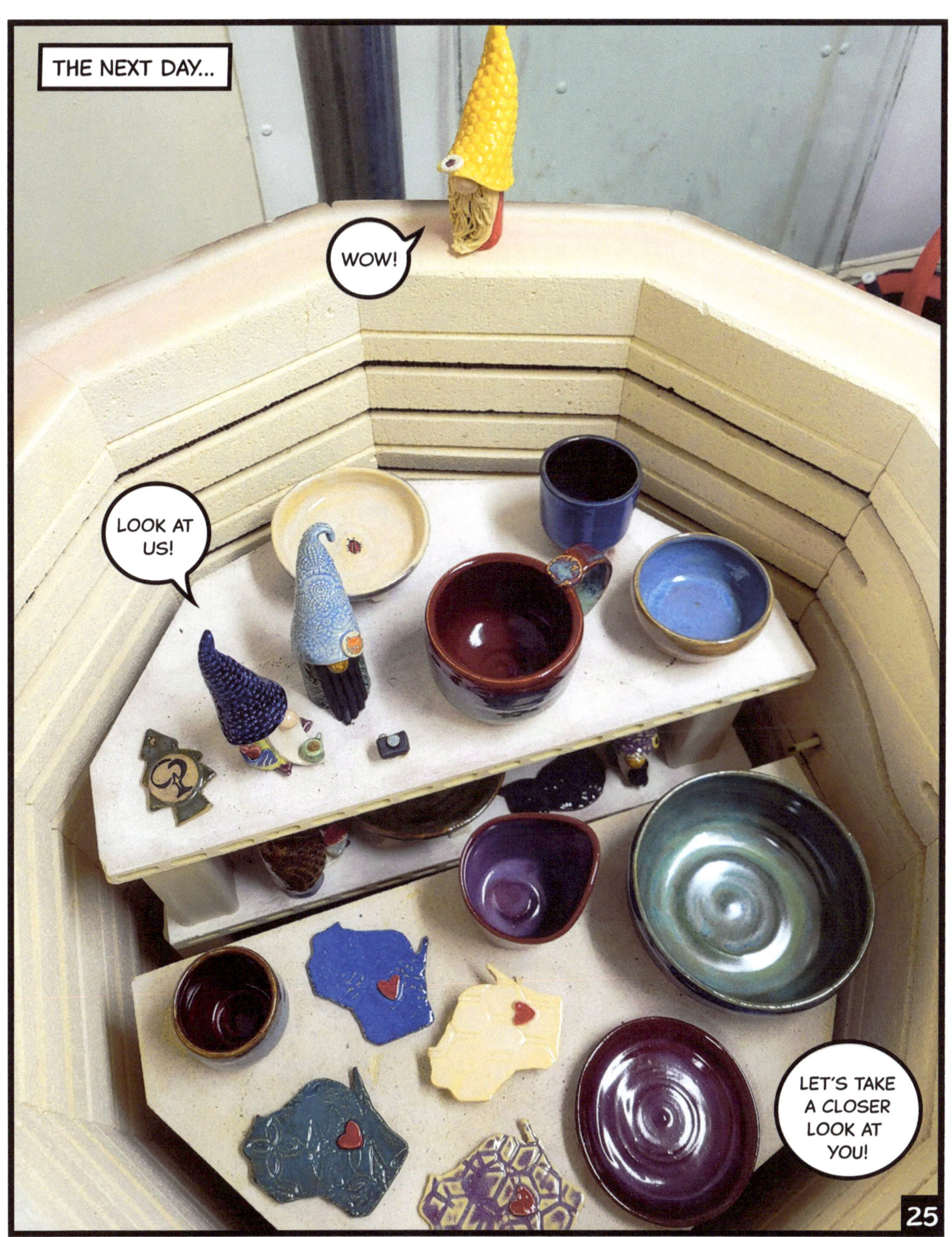

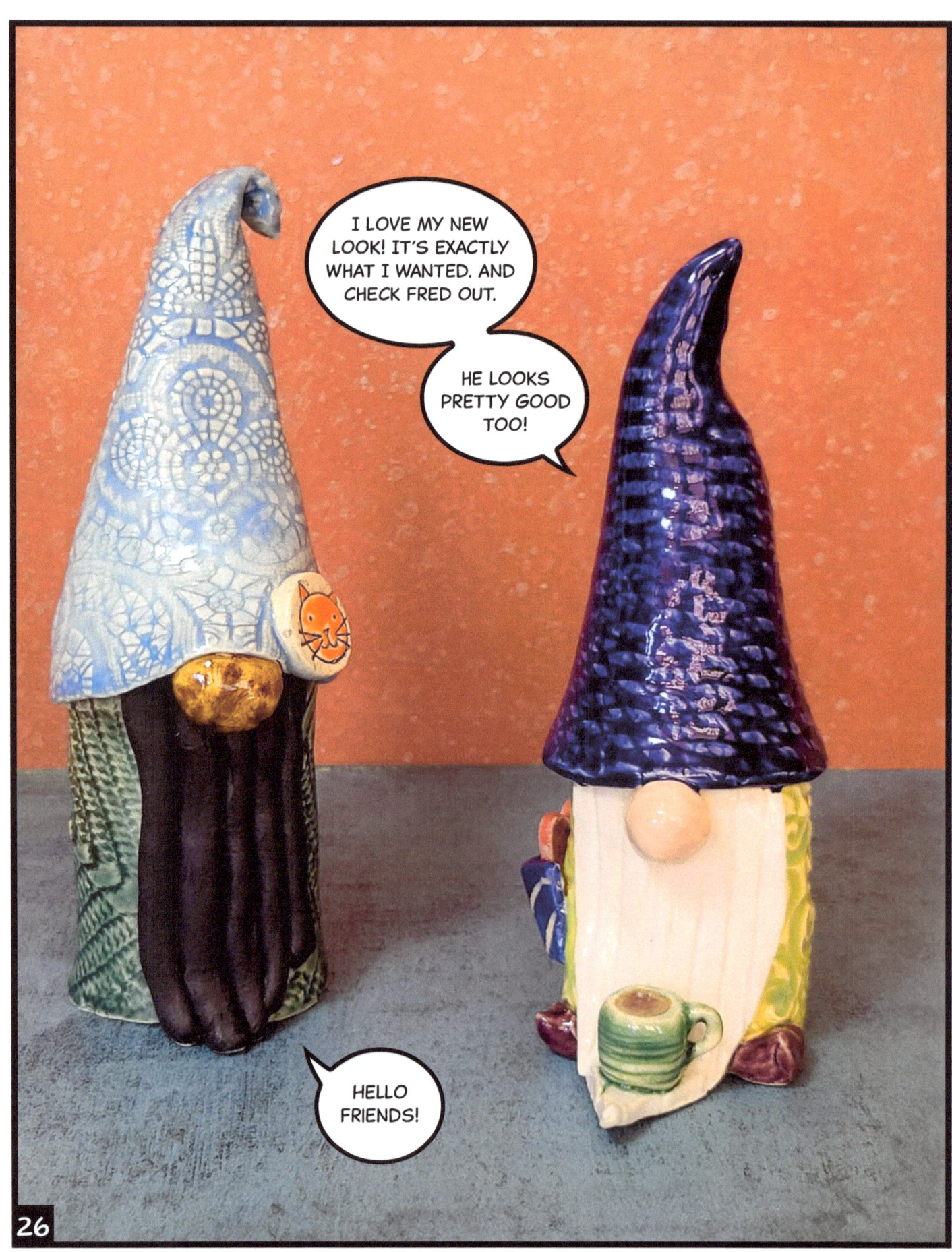

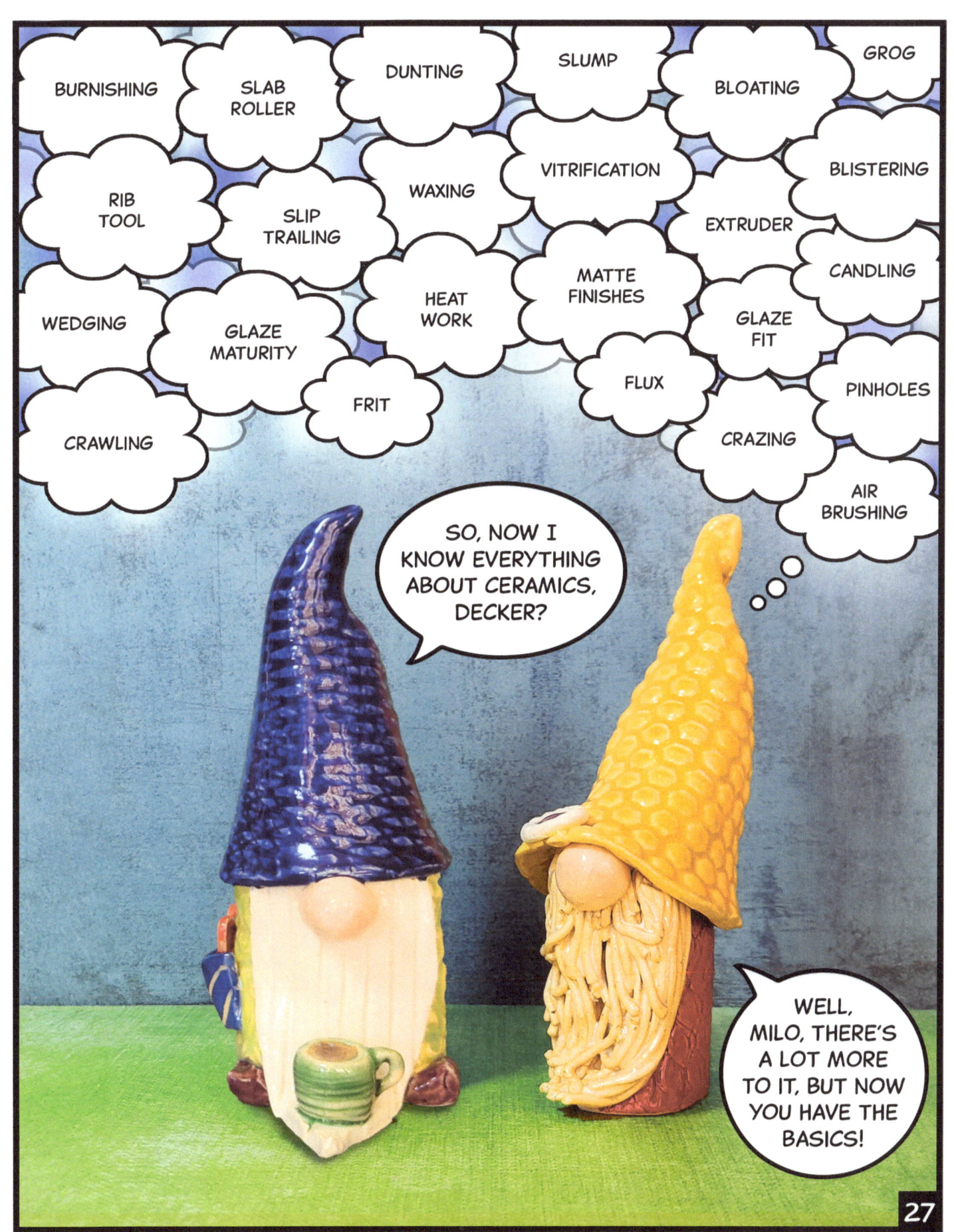

GLOSSARY

BISQUE OR BISQUEWARE - CERAMICS THAT HAVE BEEN FIRED ONCE WITHOUT GLAZE

BISQUE FIRE - THE FIRST FIRING OF CERAMICWARE TO MAKE IT STRONG AND READY FOR GLAZE

BONE DRY - CLAY THAT IS NO LONGER COOL TO THE TOUCH, IS AS DRY AS POSSIBLE, AND IS READY TO BE FIRED

CERAMICS - CLAY THAT HAS BEEN BAKED OR FIRED AT A HIGH TEMPERATURE

CLAY - CERAMICS CLAYS ARE WATER BASED SUBSTANCES MADE FROM CLAY MINERALS AND OTHER RAW MATERIALS

CONES - PYRAMIDS OF CERAMIC MATERIAL THAT HELP GAUGE IF A KILN HAS HEATED TO A HOT ENOUGH TEMPERATURE OVER THE RIGHT AMOUNT OF TIME TO FIRE THE POTTERY SUFFICIENTLY

DRYFOOTING - KEEPING THE BOTTOM OF A PIECE OF CERAMICS FREE OF GLAZE

FIRING - THE PROCESS OF BRINGING CLAY AND GLAZES TO A HIGH TEMPERATURE

GLAZE - A GLASSY COATING ON CERAMICS. CHANGES APPEARANCE WHEN FIRED

GLAZING - APPLYING GLAZE TO A CERAMIC ITEM. CAN BE DONE BY DIPPING THE ITEM IN GLAZE OR PAINTING GLAZE ON THE ITEM

GREENWARE - CLAY THAT HAS NOT BEEN FIRED

HANDBUILDING OR SCULPTING - CREATING CLAY OBJECTS BY HAND WITHOUT A WHEEL OR A MOLD

KILN - A THERMAL CHAMBER LIKE AN OVEN THAT HEATS TO HIGH TEMPERATURES TO CHANGE CLAY INTO CERAMICS AND MATURE GLAZES FROM THEIR PREFIRE STATE TO THE GLOSSY POSTFIRE STATE

LEATHER HARD - CLAY THAT IS FIRM AND COLD TO THE TOUCH. CANNOT BE SHAPED ANYMORE BUT CAN BE CARVED INTO

MOLD - A PLASTER FORM USED TO CREATE CERAMIC PIECES

POTTER'S WHEEL - A MACHINE WITH A HORIZONTAL DISC THAT A POTTER USES TO SHAPE WET CLAY INTO ROUND VESSELS SUCH AS A BOWL OR A POT

SAMPLE TILES - SMALL PIECES OF CERAMICS WITH DIFFERENT TEXTURES OR GLAZES TO SHOW WHAT A TEXTURE OR GLAZE WILL LOOK LIKE AFTER FIRIING

SCORE - TO SCRATCH THE SURFACE OF THE CLAY

SLIP - WET RUNNY CLAY. CAN BE USED AS POTTERY GLUE

SLIP CASTING - CREATING CERAMICS BY POURING LIQUID CLAY INTO MOLDS

STILTS - SMALL SUPPORTS USED WHEN FIRING GLAZED CERAMICS THAT KEEP THEM FROM STICKING TO THE KILN SHELF

THROWING - CREATING CERAMICS BY SHAPING CLAY ON A POTTER'S WHEEL

UNDERGLAZE - A COLORFUL COATING APPLIED TO CERAMICS AT THE GREENWARE OR BISQUE STAGE. NOT SHINY BUT CAN BE COVERED IN CLEAR OR COLORED GLAZE TO ADD A GLASSY COATING

WET/PLASTIC - CLAY THAT IS FRESH OUT OF THE BAG, SOFT, CAN BE SHAPED INTO ANYTHING

GLAZING TIPS

WHEN APPLYING GLAZE, THREE COATS ARE NEEDED TO ACHIEVE BOLD COLORS.
YOU CAN SEE THE DIFFERENCE IN THE IMAGE TO THE RIGHT.

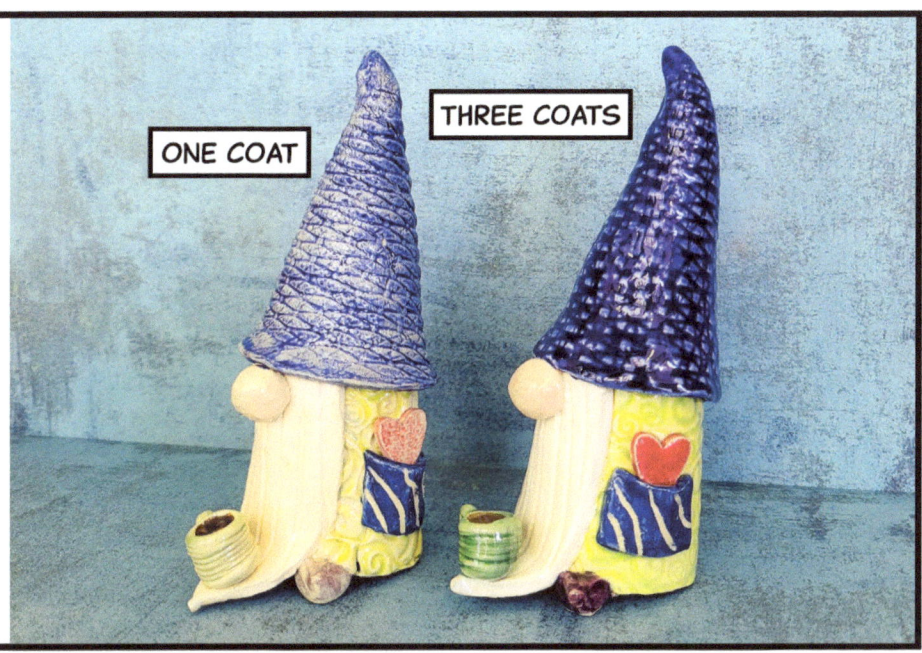

ONE COAT

THREE COATS

MISTAKES MADE WHILE GLAZING CAN BE EASY TO FIX.

A WET SPONGE CAN WASH GLAZE OFF BISQUE.

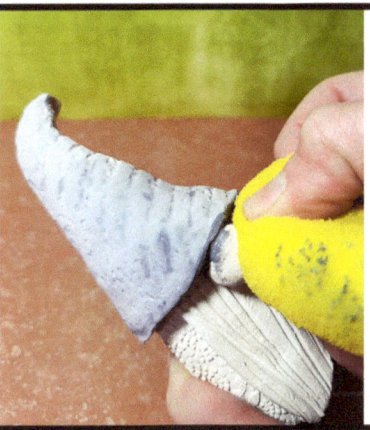

A SHARP TOOL CAN SCRAPE GLAZE OFF GLAZE.

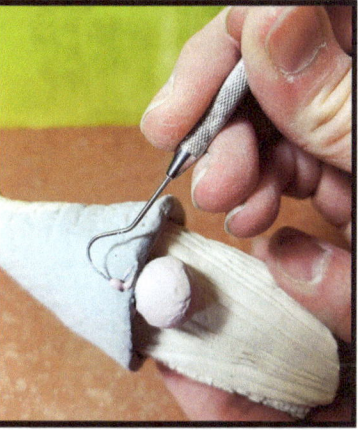

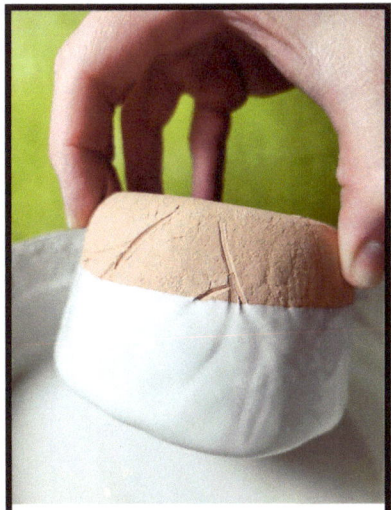

TO QUICKLY GLAZE PIECES IN A SINGLE COLOR, THE PIECES CAN BE DIPPED IN A BUCKET OF GLAZE.

TO EMPHASIZE STAMPS, LETTERING, OR TEXTURE...

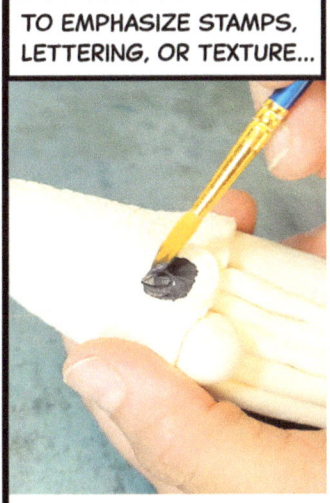

PAINT UNDERGLAZE OVER THE WHOLE AREA

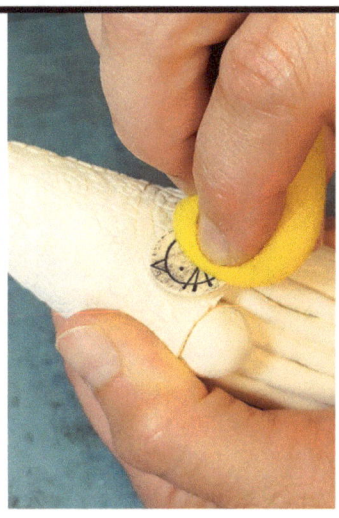

WIPE EXCESS UNDERGLAZE FROM THE SURFACE WITH A SPONGE

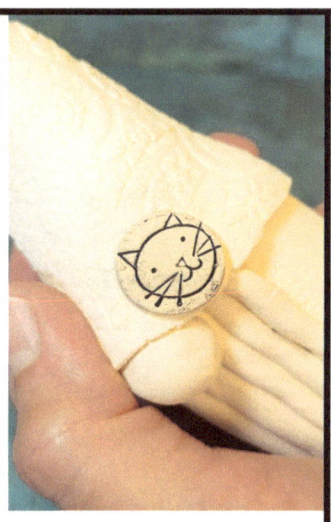

ADD CLEAR OR COLORED GLAZES ON THE SURFACE TO FINISH

CONE CHART

CONE	FAHRENHEIT	CELSIUS	
7	2262	1239	
6	2232	1222	
5	2167	1186	MIDRANGE GLAZES
4	2124	1162	
3	2106	1152	
2	2088	1142	
1	2079	1137	
01	2046	1119	
02	2016	1102	
03	1987	1086	
04	1945	1063	BISQUE
05	1888	1031	
06	1828	998	LOW FIRE GLAZES
07	1789	976	

THIS SIMPLIFIED CONE CHART SHOWS THE TEMPERATURES AND CONES DISCUSSED IN *A GNOME'S GUIDE TO CERAMICS*.

- MOST CLAY WILL BISQUE FIRE TO CONE 04.

- ONCE BISQUE FIRED, MANY LOW FIRE CLAYS AND GLAZES THEN FIRE TO THE LOWER CONE 06. MIDFIRE CLAYS AND GLAZES WILL FIRE TO CONE 5 OR 6.

- MAKE SURE TO CHOOSE A GLAZE THAT FIRES TO THE SAME TEMPERATURE AS THE CLAY. AS YOU CAN SEE IN THE CHART, CONE 06 IS VERY DIFFERENT FROM CONE 6.

CLAY CHART

THERE ARE MANY DIFFERENT VARIETIES OF CLAY. TO THE RIGHT IS A CHART SHOWING FOUR CLAY BODIES AND HOW EACH APPEARS AT DIFFERENT STATES OF THE CERAMIC PROCESS.

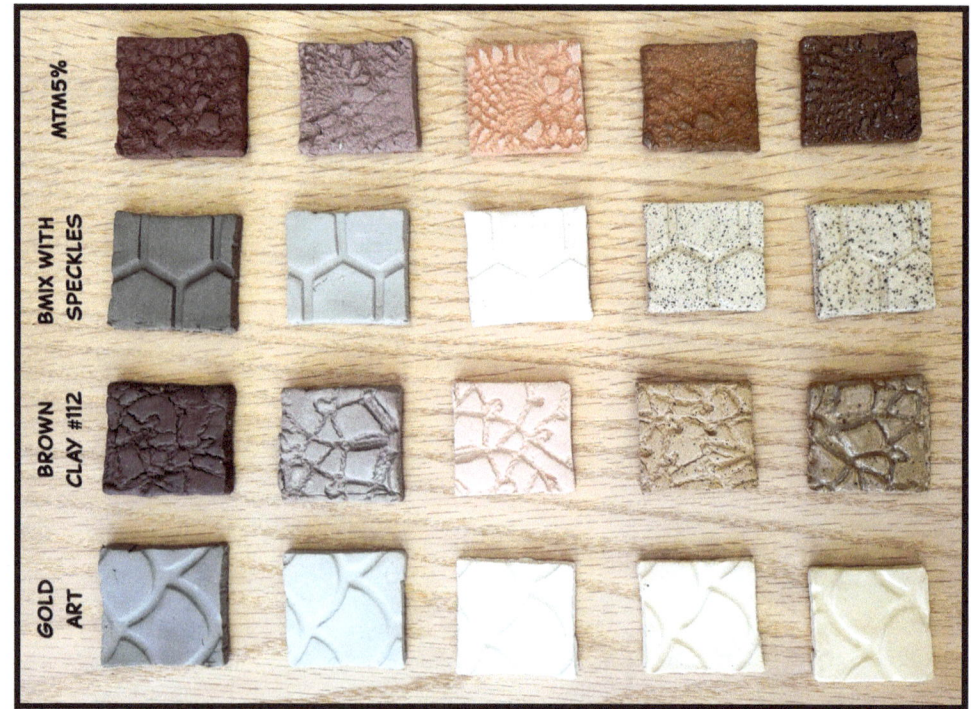

"A BIG THANK YOU TO EVERYONE WHO GAVE FEEDBACK, INSIGHTS, AND ENCOURAGEMENT AS WE EDITED THIS BOOK!"

BECKY WEIDNER
AUTHOR

BECKY WEIDNER IS AN ARTIST, AUTHOR, AND INSTRUCTOR. SHE LIVES WITH HER FAMILY IN COLUMBUS, WISCONSIN WHERE SHE SHARES HER STUDIO, *THE WORKSHOP*, WITH THE COMMUNITY THROUGH CLASSES, FIELD TRIPS, AND OTHER EVENTS. SHE HAS A PASSION FOR EXPLAINING ART PROCESSES TO BEGINNERS AND ENCOURAGING PEOPLE TO TRY NEW MEDIUMS.

"AND THANK YOU TO EVERYONE WHO HELPED ME WITH DESIGN AND LAYOUT!"

KARA GINTHER
CREATIVE DESIGN

KARA GINTHER IS AN ARTIST, DESIGNER AND STORYTELLER. SHE LIVES IN COLUMBUS, WISCONSIN AND LOVES TEACHING ART CLASSES AT *THE WORKSHOP* WITH BECKY. SHE IS ESPECIALLY EXCITED ABOUT CREATING FUN AND IMMERSIVE ENVIRONMENTS THAT INSPIRE CREATIVITY AND ENCOURAGE NEW WAYS OF THINKING.

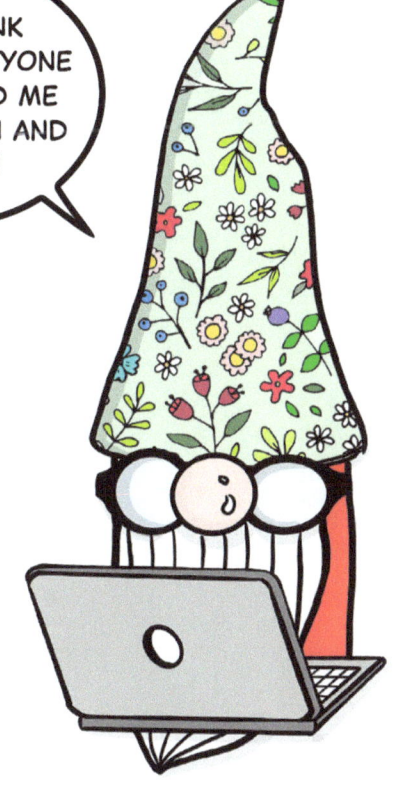

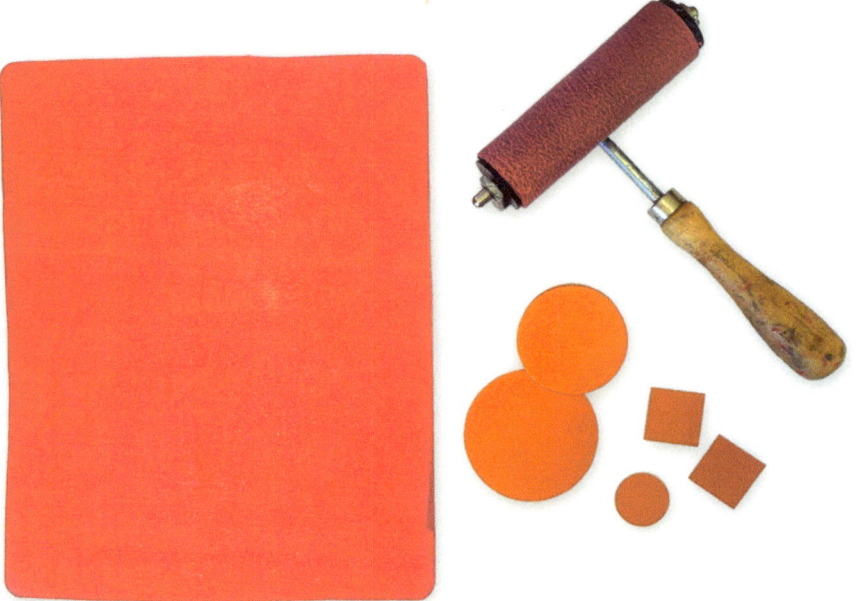
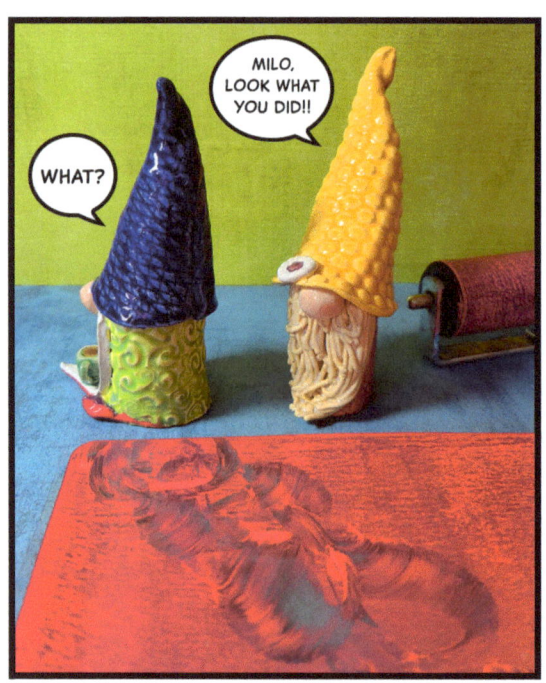
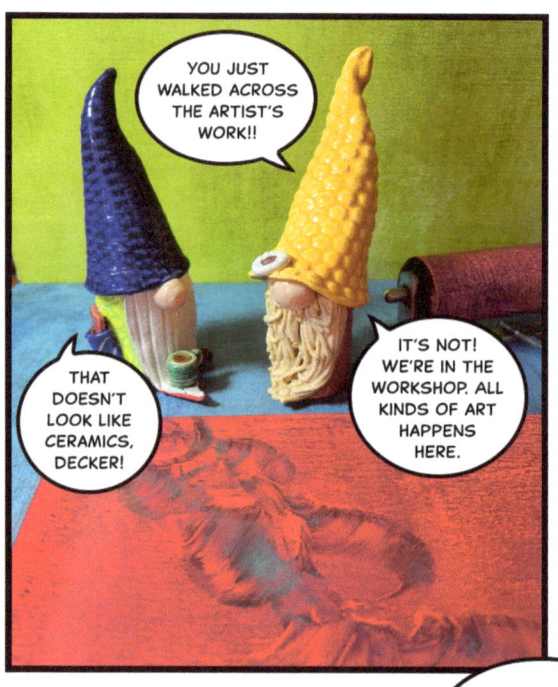